MY SEVEN SUMMITS

"A Stroke is Upon Me"

by

Mark S. Cornwall

MY SEVEN SUMMITS

"A Stroke is Upon Me"

by

Mark S. Cornwall

The above-entitled book, written by Mark S. Cornwall, was copyrighted in 2025 by Mark S. Cornwall and printed and manufactured in the United States of America. All rights to this book and its content are reserved and may not be reproduced in any form or by any electronic or mechanical means, including information storage and retrieval systems, without permission in writing from the publisher, except for a reviewer who may quote brief passages for the pleasure of their readers.

    All publishing information or other inquiries should be directed to Baby Boomer Publishing, P.O. Box 646, Summerland, California 93067.

Visit our website:

MarkCornwall.com

Dedicated to:

Mike Larrabee, for his everlasting imprint he made on me,

(...and my beautiful wife D'Arcy, who makes life one big adventure.)

PREFACE
Dick Bass's *Seven Summits*

"I have climbed the highest mountain on six of the seven continents."

This statement is steeped in controversy the moment it falls from your lips. Because no one will ever agree which peaks truly count as the Seven Summits. Two of them might not even sit on the continent they claim to represent. And who are these experts that determine the Seven Summits? What does it mean to say, "I climbed?" Does it mean I attempted, reached the summit, or simply turned back alive? Why the obsession with the tallest peaks at all? And why only six?

Modern folk hero and silver-tongued devil, Dick Bass, author of the book, *Seven Summits* (1985), chose the most popular and widely accepted geographical choice for the highest mountain on the Australian Continent: Mt. Kosciuszko at 7,310 feet. By climbing Mt. Kosciuszko, he capped off his 1983 bid to capture all seven continental summits in a single year. Unfortunately, he failed to capture one of the summits within the year when he turned back from Mt. Everest that spring. But Bass completed his quest by arranging a do-over of Everest in 1985, that launched him into the public eye as a maverick of the mountains by being first to stand atop such a particular legacy: *Seven Summits*.

These days, most young climbers never heard of him. Which is peculiar because Bass really was the seminal character in making the Seven Summit challenge a reality.

For Bass, the Seven Summits are: Kosciuszko for Australia, Mt. Everest for Asia, Mt. Elbrus for Europe, Denali for North America, Aconcagua for South America, Kilimanjaro for Africa and Vinson Massif for Antarctica.

Since completing his book *Seven Summits*, the term continent grew in its meaning. It used to mean "a landmass surrounded by oceans," but then science revealed that beneath the sea of this 'island continent' of Australia there were submerged continental shelves. New theories on the evolution of tectonic plates, and other geographic discoveries spurred debates over who owns what new indigenous lands.

This changing opinion also affected some elite mountaineers who used their world celebrity to postulate a new replacement for Mt. Kosciuszko, Australia, as one of the Seven Summits. Two of the world's most elite climbers, Reinhold Messner of Austria, and Pat Morrow of Canada, took umbrage with Bass's choice of Mt. Kosciuszko, treating the victory party for his Seven Summits as though it was a publicity stunt, claiming the "easy hike" up 7,310 feet was not worthy of being the highest mountain on the Australian Continent.

This conclusion was perhaps provoked by Bass's *Seven Summits* documentary, wherein his entourage of merry makers celebrated their victory by driving a limo up the dirt road through Rawson Pass to within a few meters of the summit of Mt. Kosciuszko and walking up. They were dressed in formal attire, tuxedos and gowns, including black hats and gold masks, and sipped champagne as they strolled to the top.

Reinhold Messner brought a buzz kill to this party when, based on his *Ubermensche* resume of conquering the world's most wicked summits, he declared the highest mountain in Australia is in Indonesia. But what was his motive?

Messner's list of Seven Summits replaced Kosciuszko with Carstensz Pyramid, a 16,024-foot mountain on the jungle island of New Guinea. At the time, New Guinea was commonly referred to as part of Southeast Asia. But in 1978, when Messner first claimed Carstensz Pyramid was part of Australasia, he had just climbed

Carstensz Pyramid and was celebrated for having climbed six of the seven summits. Without Mt. Kosciuszko on his list anymore, he had only Vincent Massif in Antarctica to complete all seven.

Messner's authority came from geologists who theorized New Guinea was pushed up from the rim of Australia's continental shelf, long ago, when the Australian tectonic plate collided with the Eurasian tectonic plate. That was good enough for Messner in 1978, but in 1983 the world opinion demanded he climb Kosciuszko to be recognized for climbing six of the seven summits. He went back and did it and consequently was tied with Bass.

Boys will be boys, right? But change the Seven Summits? What's up with calling the New Guinea, culturally and ecologically considered part of Southeast Asia, a part of Down Under? Patrick Morrow, another ambitious climber chimed in, "Being a climber first and a collector second, I felt strongly that Carstensz Pyramid, the highest mountain in Australasia ... was a true mountaineer's objective."

Whaaat!? Morrow's statement begs two questions. What is a "mountaineer's objective" and, who is a "mountaineer collector?"

Morrow ignores the fact that Dick Bass's celebrity from *Seven Summits* contributed more to the popularity of

PREFACE

climbing mountains than Morrow and Messner contributed over their combined lives. Bass opened the quest for Seven Summits to the world, giving birth to a new age of discovery through mountaineering. The dream of climbing mountains and conquering their summits is the true mountaineer's objective, not "collecting" them.

When Bass conquered the Seven Summits he gave every armchair climber in America the inspiration to believe that they too could climb all seven of the world's continental peaks. Bass's dream doesn't exclude anybody from enjoying the accomplishment of this goal or trying to obtain it. And it doesn't limit the dream to an elite few, like Morrow and Messner. However, it does require a lot of time and money.

Is Morrow suggesting he strongly believes the true mountaineer wants the seventh summit of the *Seven Summits* to be more difficult than the other six? Says who? Even God commanded rest on the seventh day. Why not a walk-up for the seventh summit, it's only one? Bass showed how it could be done for fun—and Mt. Kosciuszko happens to be correctly on the Australian Continent.

The good part of this Bass/Messner debacle is it opens the debate to more choices. When considering a third choice for the highest mountain in Australasia, Mt. Cook is up there. It's the highest in the Southern Alps of New Zealand, at 12,218 feet. That makes it the highest mountain on the Australasia Continent, without having to bend the rules. This is based on the indisputable fact Mt. Cook is the highest mountain south of New Guinea's Carstensz Pyramid, making it positively the highest mountain Down Under.

You remember New Zealand, don't you, the other English-speaking nation right next to Australia, on the larger Oceania Continent, where dozens of peaks over 10,000-feet sprout up from the glaciers like giant stalagmites? The outfitter's brochure for climbing Mt. Cook showed a shiny color photo of the guide *extraordinaire* Phil Penny, just below the summit, an ice axe in each hand, front pointing his way up the 65 percent headwall. Imagine climbing a headwall like that with two ice axes. That's what mountaineering is all about, and that was good enough for me. Plus, New Zealand is beautiful to visit. It's not jungle. And it was the home of Ed Hillary.

The same type of controversy exists over whether Mt. Elbrus in Russia, is the highest mountain on the European Continent. It is not. It is an 18,513-foot peak in the Caucasus Range just *east* of Sochi, Russia, the site of the

PREFACE

2014 Winter Olympics. It lies clearly on the Asian side of Europe. I'll explain this fiasco later.

But if you climb Mt. Elbrus thinking you reached the highest point in Europe, you've been duped and should go directly to the Archipelago. Mt. Blanc, at 15,774 feet in France, has always been, and always will be the highest mountain in Europe.

Vern Tejas had his own way of resolving the controversy over which summits should be included on the list of Seven Summits. In 2010, more than two decades later, at age 57, Vern set a new world speed record for climbing all Seven Summits within 134-day period. You do that by standing on top Vincent Massif one day, and the summit of Denali 134 days later. In between, Vern followed the Bass/Messner routes that includes both Carstensz Pyramid in Indonesia, and Kosciusko in Australia, then Elbrus, Aconcagua, and Kilimanjaro, but left out the original seventh summit of Mt. Blanc, France.

Dick Bass may have been first to summit all seven, but Vern Tejas trumped him ten times over and wrote a book about it in 2017 entitled *Seventy Summits: Life in the Mountains.* Vern's way of resolving the debate was to add the errant mountain to the list and climb them all, at least ten times.

See? All it takes is time and money.

MT. EVEREST, NEPAL (1983)

1.
Bass Sets the Stage

The last time I saw Dick Bass was at the trailhead to Gor Shep in 1983 where I cheered him goodbye and good luck; but truth be known, he looked a straggler. Alone, loaded down with a full expedition pack, and a cervical collar around his neck to brace against a pinched nerve. Wracked with dysentery, he was moving slowly up the path to a party given for his benefit at Everest Base Camp.

There was bullshit coming out both orifices of Dick. His bright Texas grin was replaced with a grimace at every step. I had just come down from Base Camp the day before and thought he was in no shape to summit the highest mountain in the world. I wrote in my journal that evening: "I wish them the best of luck, but I don't think those two plastic packages have a chance in hell of getting to the summit." Remember the term *plastic*?

The pinched nerve foretold his agonizing story. All the money in the world couldn't have gotten him or his climbing partner, Frank Wells, up to 29,029 feet that year. Fortunately, Bass's injury did not affect his mouth, as he was always talking about big ideas, like the ski resort he discovered and built in Utah. Dick told me while eating dinner in Bangkok the month before about his dear friend and mentor Marty Hoey, who taught him the skill of mountain climbing. She also taught him a valuable life lesson.

Ironically, as is the nature of mountaineering, Ms. Hoey inexplicably fell out of her harness and down the north face of Everest to her death the year previous. As Bass told the story, he was sitting at a Wyoming campfire, when Marty, who barely knew him, and before he even knew what the *Seven Summits* were, told him when it came to talking about climbing mountains, he "needed to put your body behind your mouth and stop talking out your ass."

That's the lesson he no doubt reflected upon, just before he decided to journey back to Everest in 1985 to become the oldest person (at the time) to summit the world's tallest mountain at age 56. Bass took the honors of beating Messner to the punch of capturing his seventh summit while Messner sat waiting for a chance to climb Vinson Massif, which never came. Thus, Bass became King of the Seven Summits in the fall of 1985 and beat Reinhold Messner.

MT. EVEREST

When Dick Bass failed to summit Mt. Everest in 1983, he learned the hardest lesson mountaineering can teach you, other than death, and that is: disappointment. Regardless of how many mountains you climbed, or how hard you try, or how important it is, or what tragedy may befall you if you fail, or even if you regard it as the most sacred act of your life — if the summit isn't meant to be yours, you won't get it that time. That's what makes conquering all seven summits so difficult. The expense of time and money in going back for more.

Take Bass for example. One of the richest men in the world, who had everything, until he was denied the summit of his dreams. The summits are not for sale. Bass had only Mt. Kosciuszko left when he was refused Everest. There was nothing he could do but live with the crushing defeat. The disappointment of being one mountain short is something I feel every day. But Bass had the resources to do something about it.

Bass and I spent the night in Periche at about 16,500 feet. I was coming down and he was going up to Gor Shep, the last stop before Everest Base Camp. That previous night I spent a mile above Gor Shep in a stone walled refuge with my three sherpas. The refuge was just high enough for me to squeeze through the opening with a plastic sheet as a door to sit inside to feel protected.

Syla, my non-English speaking sherpa guide, and my last two porters, were my companions. No climber should be without his cook and water boy, and they'd been with me for over a month, since we set off from Katmandu.

We started out as one big happy family of six. There was the Sahib (me), and five Sherpa natives who gently served me in exactly the manner their forefathers had been taught by the gentlemen who did reconnaissance for the English. For decades, their care in the Himalayas assured me a pot of steaming hot water every morning, after being awakened by the water boy who joyously announced, "Good morning sir, hot water for you!" Sometimes he would hike five miles down to the river to fetch water so he could present it in his grand fashion, and I could wash my face.

We began the expedition on a crowded light blue and silver bus that broke down 15 miles outside Katmandu. That's where we started trekking, 170 miles from our destination. Our 200-mile trek across the fingers of the Himalayan range began at 3,000-feet, then we climbed as high as 13,000-feet, before descending into the next valley and crossing the river again on yet another suspension bridge. We sometimes did this routine three times a day during our 15-day journey to the Khumbu Valley. That's the valley made famous by Sir Edmund Hillary.

Most climbers going to Mt. Everest fly straight to Lukla's 9,000-foot airport, then trek up the river heading north to Namche Bazaar, then Tengboche, and beyond to Everest. I trekked from Katmandu to Everest Base Camp because that was the best way to acclimatize myself for my solo ascent of Mt. Everest without oxygen.

I also love being in faraway places and enjoy the style of travel. It's romantic to remember the sherpa baking pea bread over the fire and sharing home brewed Ratzi wine with my guides. But it's somewhat painful to remember the dysentery and hangovers that follow.

The morning before running into Dick Bass in Periche, I awoke in the refuge hut at 18,000 with my three companions who had grown unhappy with our expedition as we ascended. We were now at Everest's front door. From out of nowhere a blizzard blew in. I sat on the floor with my back against the stones, near the entrance to the tiny hut, and looked at the ragged lot that stuck with me. The snow was in a maniacal dance outside the doorway, just a foot away. I watched the flakes twisting and turning through the slit of plastic sheet serving as a door. It was so bright outside I had to turn away from looking out at whiteness.

For heat, there was a tiny kerosene stove which the sherpas cranked up and huddled around every few minutes. The key adjective here is "tiny" because next to *these* mountains any effort man can exert to overcome the obstacle of cold is tiny in comparison. We were camping at 18,000 feet, and outside the plastic sheet lay another 12,000 feet of snow-covered Mt. Everest.

My sherpas wanted to get off the mountain and who could blame them. Squatting on their haunches, bunched around that tiny kerosene burner, only one of them had a sweater, the other, a thin Levi's jacket. I had five layers of clothing, a huge down jacket, two pairs of thick wool socks, boots, a cap and a jacket over my legs. I was holding my thick wool sweater in reserve and had given my old jacket to Syla. The cook had no socks on under his Converse shoes, and the water boy wore leather shoes older than he was.

When I returned to Katmandu after the climb, I complained about their situation to their outfitter. He told me the sherpas customarily sell their mountain gear in preference of money. They give no thought toward suffering consequently. "They like to suffer," the outfitter said.

The Big Storyteller

Dick Bass is a big, big, BIG, storyteller. Sharing tales is as much a part of mountaineering as brewing a cup of tea, but Dick takes it to the next level. Being a man of grand enterprises, Bass prided himself on his illustrious oral accounts thereof. He's a great storyteller, but don't think that doesn't come without practice. The stories he practiced on me and others that night in Periche were the same stories he regaled me with at dinner in Bangkok on March 18, 1983. I remember the date because it was my birthday. I turned 33 years old.

We were the only two passengers on our flight from the U.S. who were looking for something to eat at the stopover hotel at 4:00 in the morning. I noticed Bass earlier on the plane flying tourist class during the 15-hour flight from Seattle to Bangkok. He moved freely about the cabin from seat to seat visiting with other passengers. He was the only person on the flight who drank more Scotch than me, and I was taking advantage of the free pour from a beautiful Thai stewardess. What impressed me most about Bass was the way he was followed seat to seat by a rotating bevy of female passengers. Who is this guy?

The restaurant was a modern well-lighted place that left a nice first impression for my first time in Thailand. I sat at a separate table, not far from where he was and thought, hey, there's that guy again. Looking around, he engaged me with that big Texas grin and said, "Where you going?"

I said, "I'm going to climb Mt. Everest."

He said, "I have the permit to climb Mt. Everest."

I said, "Do you mind if I join you?"

In 1983 the Nepalese government issued only one permit for an expedition to climb in the Spring, and another for an expedition in the Fall. If you were not on the team with the permit you were not allowed to climb on Everest. Bass had the wherewithal to finance the original permit holder's expedition, making it his own. And that earned him, and his climbing partner Frank Wells, the privilege of attempting Mt. Everest that year, same as he did again in 1985. That included about fifty sherpas and other climbers with him. There was nothing fair about it, but what did I care? I was sitting with the man that had the permit. But it didn't work out that way.

I found out we had something else very much in common, other than climbing Everest. We both were *aficionados* of the awe-inspiring works of adventurer/author Richard Halliburton, the quintessential "Dreamer, Traveler, Poet, *Bon Vivant.*" I read all his books starting with *Seven League Boots* and *New Worlds to Conquer,* while going to UC Santa Barbara, and living in the library.

Halliburton was an American explorer in the 1920's and 30's, who climbed the Matterhorn, went to Fuji, climbed Mt. Olympus, swam the Panama Canal, as well as the Hellespont channel in Greece, flew an airplane around the world, worked cargo ships, and had the most bizarre experience in Communist Russia; then supported himself by writing books about his adventures. That was the person I wanted to be (and so did Dick Bass).

I celebrated my graduation from college *a la* Halliburton, by coming up with the best travel adventure I could think of. First, I needed money. I headed north to Alaska to work high-lead logging, then south to explore the full length of the Amazon River. I fell in love with a Brazilian goddess at *Carnaval* in Salvador Bahia, then crisscrossed the South American Continent like the Great Liberator, *Simon Bolivar,* whose statue graces every city plaza along the way. I took the bus from Rio, the death train to Santa Cruz, a steamer across *Lake Titicaca,* the Inca Trail to *Machu Picchu*, hitchhiked the Andes to Bogota, flew back to La Paz, Bolivia, trained and bussed to *Garganta del Diablo* (Iguazu Falls), then wrote a book about it in two months in Buenos Aires called *The Fool's Folly*.

Dick Bass idolized Richard Halliburton's call to adventure so much he allowed his life to imitate art and copied him. Just as Halliburton followed in the footsteps of mythical Odysseus to travel the trail of Hellenistic Greece, Bass dropped out of his corporate lifestyle to follow in Haliburton's footsteps and swim the Hellespont Channel in Greece. Bass ran the original route of Pheidippides, from Marathon to Athens, and traced a host of Halliburton inspired adventures, while taking the Bass family on a trip around the world.

I assumed Bass had begun his exploits of Odysseus' feats the same way Halliburton had, by first climbing Mt. Olympus to greet the mythical Zeus before venturing on to swim the Hellespont. But I was wrong, Bass didn't bother to climb Olympus. I chuckled to myself because I had climbed Mt. Olympus in 1972, as an alternative to attending the '72 Olympics. It was my homage to Halliburton, if you know what I mean.

MT. EVEREST, NEPAL (1983)

2.

How to Explain It All

I awoke to the freshest, clearest, and bluest view of Mt. Everest that I had ever seen. I threw open the flap of my tent and there it was, in all its glory. It was freezing, of course, but after yesterday it was a welcome calm, spread like whipped cream over the terrain.

This was our chance to make a run for Base Camp. With Syla as my guide, we trekked up the Khumbu Glacier to its end at the base of Mt. Everest. Sometimes you forget, by looking at pictures and movies of Everest showing the pageantry of climbers across the plateau, you begin to think there must be a steady line of sherpas and tourists meandering up the glacier, bringing supplies and photographing events of the day.

But that's not how it was in 1983. There was only one group of climbers on the moraine, and they were Bass's. Nobody else went out there because it's in the death zone. In fact, you've been in the death zone since you left Periche, the last habitable village at 16,500-feet. From there, we went to Gor Shep and slept in the "tiny" stone refuge. And now Syla is leading me up the glacier to its very end at the Everest Base Camp at the foot of the Khumbu Icefall at 18,500 feet.

The Icefall marks the gateway to the technical climb of Mt. Everest.

The 1983 Base Camp was placed a couple of crevasses away from the front of the Icefall. I've seen photographs of how it looks today, and it looks nothing like the Icefall 40 years ago, thanks to global warming. But, just like the Sherpa who grew up surrounding the Khumbu Glacier, the culture has also gently receded. You'll never see the original Sherpa tribe again.

Only me, two men, and one boy were left in my expedition. We were camped a mile above Gor Shep, preferring the solitude of the climb over sharing a room with the tourists. The cook, the water boy and Syla, shared the tiny stone room. I slept as usual in my *one-man* tent – really, it was for "one man."

The very first night we camped out on our expedition there were five sherpas with me. Syla insisted I sleep in the big tent they brought for me, a tent big enough for all six of us. Where were they going to sleep? I didn't really think about it. But when I got up to piss, I found all six of them crammed into my one-man tent; how they did it mystifies me. But they were all in there. We made the switch for the remainder of the trip and felt much better about it.

Syla and I only got lost once on our run to Base Camp, which was commendable given the fact new snow covered any trace of a trail. It was difficult to follow the trail even when there was no snow covering it. I trudged along for what seemed like five miles after Syla left me, charging ahead to make sure he could find the trail to base camp. I followed his tracks one after the other. The altitude was problematic for me at 18,000 feet, even though the scale of the climb was gradually uphill, the smallest rise seemed exhausting.

Slowly, I made my way up the moraine, and it wasn't until I got curious enough to do so that I decided to investigate the cracks in the ice I was stepping over. I got down on one knee and peered into the fissure, down deep into the blue/green. What I found was a turquoise cavern.

Was I crossing a bottomless crevasse? I looked up and suddenly became aware of my surroundings. I was in a field of gigantic stalagmites, twelve feet high, pushing up from the ice below. I couldn't believe it. Stalagmites sprouting all around me. I looked back down the hole through the six-inch crack in the moraine and saw the ruptured blue, deep aquamarine you can only see between slices of glacier, like gargoyles and hedgehogs. I was standing in a gargantuan ice garden that gives seeds to stalagmites and crevasses. The sun was shining so brightly, I could barely see. I wanted to walk with my eyes closed, even though I was wearing black sunglasses.

Pressing on towards Base Camp I had a rude awakening brought on by my trusted guide. I could see Syla standing on the distant horizon, maybe a quarter mile away. This was a good sign; I figured he had the camp in sight. And it was about time! Stepping up the pace, I huffed and puffed to the same ridge where he was standing, only to discover it was on a false horizon.

One of those horizon's where you're saying, "It's gotta be over the next ridge," and you get to the next ridge, only to see ten more ridges, but no Base Camp, meaning you've still got a long way to go. We'd been two hours into this trek, and I couldn't believe the camp was that far away. You could see the damn icefall right in front of you. Hell, everybody makes it to Base Camp, don't they? I looked at Syla and he said, I swear to God:

"This is it. This is Base Camp. Right here."

I looked around incredulously. "What do you mean? There's no camp here." I looked around again to see if I was missing anything.

"Yes, yes, this is Base Camp. It's right over there," he said, waving his arm over the general area, indicating where the camp was. "Yes. This is Base Camp."

I liked Syla. We had become friends despite our language barrier, but this was too much. Did he expect me to believe him, without the benefit of a single tent, which would have been humorous? But if he believed my desire to get to Base Camp was left up to his laziness or frustration in finding the trail, well, he was sorely mistaken. I was insulted. I smirked at him and took off by myself towards the Icefall. Like I really needed a guide!

Getting Beyond Base Camp

The trek over the moraine from Gor Shep to Base Camp would be difficult for anyone because of the 18,000 ft. altitude. Whether it was a climber of renowned, or any regular Jane, it's simply not meant to be habitable. The climbers trekking to Base Camp as a precursor to challenging Everest—unless they're of the ilk of Reinhold Messner or Vern Tejas—are just men and women in very good shape. What must be different about them if they plan on summiting is their mental "attitude." I always hated that word. But call it mindset or temperament, you still need the right one.

They've got to have the determination to press on with the ordeal—press on and on and on with no doubt or questions as to why, or if it's worth it. To have the correct mindset, your goal must be clear. You must feel the climb is vital to the soul and hearts of Man, but most assuredly, vital to *you*.

At about 16,000 feet you'll realize what it means to have the *guts* to keep going. When your will fails you, and your better judgment tells you to stop, that's when the sport of mountain climbing begins. There's no air to breathe freely, so you begin to fight for oxygen. The first element of the mind to vanish is the imagination. There's not enough oxygen to spend any of it humoring you with daydreams. Then feelings of love and hate disappear, there seems to be no oxygen for that either. For now, it's one foot in front of the other, your steps and breath harmonizing a lovely mantra. You become mesmerized by the rhythm of your motion, and whatever mantra you created to feel strong.

You may have wondered what it would be like climbing with a group of professional climbers? Each one testing their mettle against the other, competing for strength, aching to be the best. But that's not how it plays out at 18,000 feet or more. One of them may feel strong *that day,* while the other will be shuffling his feet, hacking up phlegm and having a hard time of it. But they keep on rollin' and don't stop.

Everybody suffers on the climb. The winners learn to live with it and move on. All these injuries can be thought of as one big scab. You live with it getting knocked off and scabbing over day after day. But that doesn't affect the climb because it *is* the climb. Scabs don't matter. Tweaked knees and gobs of phlegm are no longer personalized. They're part of the whole climb, up and down the mountain. It's all one big obstacle to be endured, unified, and overcome.

At any rate, when I arrived at Everest Base Camp, my dreams came tumbling down. I was glad I hadn't made these few scattered tents my home for the next six weeks. It was a lonely cloister of tents against a mighty frozen backdrop. This was a *tent outpost* on the fringe of the world, owned by Dick Bass. It wasn't the "city of tents" you'd find there today, with 600 climbers scrambling around to find a Sani-Hut. In this tent outpost there were perhaps fifty sherpa sleeping in twenty-five tents, and fifteen international climbers staying in bigger tents, all on one permit for the Spring season, March through June. It's one permit for the privilege of climbing Mt. Everest. One permit for everybody. If you wanted to climb you had to be in the party with the permit. That was the law.

This wasn't fair, but let's face it, in 1983 there weren't that many people in the world interested in climbing Mt. Everest. And it wasn't Dick Bass's permit per se, but he had the money, and that bought him the opportunity to climb. Unfortunately, he failed in his 1983 bid to summit but came back two years later to buy himself another opportunity, upon which he capitalized. That's how Dick Bass became personally responsible for opening the doors of opportunity to those 600 climbers who think Mt. Everests is in their destiny.

I looked out over those tents and didn't see myself. No way did I have the patience to wait my turn. The process of being invited to join the team was fanciful. "Hey, Dick, mind if I join your expedition?" Last I heard that cost money. On top of that, getting chosen for the summit team by someone I didn't know made it virtually impossible. That's how it worked. But when it came down to it...well, I don't know.

MT. EVEREST

There I was, at the right time and place, in late April of 1983. It was just as I planned, but my motivation eluded me. I didn't feel like finding Dick Bass and cajoling him into letting me participate with his team. Maybe I burned myself out by trekking from Katmandu to Base Camp, but that's no excuse. I used that 200-mile jaunt across the Himalayas to acclimatize, and there was no doubt I was in the best shape of my life. No, I was physically prepared, but not mentally. There was something else...maybe I didn't fit in?

This *was* my first big climb, and I'd never done a "technical climb" before. No, that wasn't the problem. Standing there, surveying the camp and its citizens, what I saw was a fucking circus that would have driven me nuts. It seemed doomed to fail.

When Syla and I first approached Base Camp from the edge of camp, the man's words were, "Could you please accommodate us by staying on the perimeter of the camp because of the sherpa's ..."

Say no more, that was all the greeting I needed to hear. Not friendly. The sherpas (plural) were conducting their Puji ceremony; a traditional Buddhist offering of goat's blood to the gods in return for Sherpa safe keeping. So apparently it was time for them to get serious about the task at hand, i.e., climbing Mt. Everest. But *not* time for everybody.

There was a group of fifteen to twenty dedicated sherpas huddled in a sacred circle of prayer, begging for their life, asking for safety and delivery from evil. Meanwhile, thirty yards away, was another group of sherpas blasting soul music from their stereo. This gave me serious misgivings about the unification of the team.

Who are these guys? Aren't they sherpas too? They were younger men laughing and joking through the Puji ceremony, not giving a respectable hoot toward their elder's sacred sacrament of the Puji. This show of no respect gave the ceremony the distinct fragrance of superficiality—like they were play acting in front of the cameras, blowing smoke in each other's faces.

A set of colorful flags were strung from a pole at the center of the circle, strung out amongst the Sherpa in prayer wheel form. But the rock music hammering in the background made the scene seem cheeky. Then came the final coup de gras: the scent of marijuana came wafting through on the airwaves of *Stairway to Heaven*. Why didn't the man come over and tell the boys, "Could you please accommodate us and turn that shit off"?

MT. EVEREST

The Sherpa as a Nepalese tribe have become the foundation for all modern Himalayan back packing expeditions. The English aristocracy organized, trained and taught them how to execute their duties in exactly the manner they do today. The British Military, using the same moral superiority with which they ruled the Indian Empire with for eighty-nine years, from 1858 to 1947, could see the Sherpa value in their capacity for endurance and ability to carry heavy loads at altitude. Naturally, they sought to exploit it.

The Sherpa are native to Nepal, stemming from a Tibetan tribe that settled in the Khumbu Region of Nepal, the region encircling the southern approaches to Mt. Everest which sits on the Tibetan/Nepalese border. They have a cultural disposition that allows them to "embrace with magnanimity and apparent calm, all the vicissitudes of life." In other words, they were "happy campers" all the time. Plus, the Sherpa could *persevere* beyond all others, were loyal to the cause, and disciplined in their manner. Perfect for the military.

But what the English loved most about the sherpas was the way they worked for cheap. The burden of their loads far outweighed the earnings they were paid. And therein lies the pushback by today's sherpa. Those young men smoking marijuana have grown up, and their sons and daughters want to make *real* money. It's a business today, not an opportunity for sherpas to show off their inherent cultural skills.

MT. EVEREST, NEPAL (1983)

3.

Making Friends – Sort Of

You'll never forget the first time you see Everest. You can only see its pyramidal face glittering from Base Camp. No luck trying to see it from anyplace else along the Khumbu. One day me and my new friend Mike Dunlop decided to get a better look at that pyramidal glitter from the other side of the glacier. You get a full-frontal view of Everest by climbing Kala Patthar.

Kala Patthar sits directly opposite Mt. Everest on the glacier plane. From atop Kala Patthar, you get to view the Everest Mountain Range, so to speak, including Nuptse, Lohste, and Changtse, those three 26,000-foot peaks sitting in front of Everest. Beautifully chiseled, they make the ideal entourage for their big friend. Further south stands the "Matterhorn of the Himalayas," the most visually striking mountain in the world, Mt. Ama Dablam. But this spectacular stand-alone mountain still falls 6,528 feet short of Everest at 22,349-feet. Mt. Everest stands alone in solemn grandeur.

Mike and I met on the trail from Katmandu. He was a Canadian from the Yukon, who drove an emergency medical ambulance. Mike was out exploring the world. I forget how we met, but neither of us had spoken English for over a week, so when we met, we had one thing in common—we were the only guys speaking English.

We had a lot to talk about too. From women to Nirvana, sports to politics, auto parts to woodshop, the friendly banter went on and on. We made an odd-looking couple, seeing as though I was a head taller than him, but that guy wasted no time smelling the roses. He couldn't wait for anything. We ended up trekking all the way from Namche to Kala Patthar and back, but it was always off and on, like "I'll see you later."

Mike was not a part of my expedition and therefore relegated to sleeping in the guest cottages filled with other tourist climbers. This wasn't so bad, but for some strange reason, guest lodges had no chimneys for their fireplaces. No chimney means the smoke is left to linger in the living room filled with tired, sweaty climbers. The smoke tries to find its way out through cracks in thick walls, or under the door. This led to one irrefutable fact: Mike was eating and sleeping in a room so filled with smoke it would burn your eyes.

MT. EVEREST

I, on the other hand, was sleeping in the lap of luxury. Traveling with my five-man Nepalese team assured me acceptance in every circle of Himalayan life. With the sherpa by my side, taking care of every detail of the trek from Katmandu, I was welcome to set my one-man tent anywhere. At the loneliest home on the terrace, where grandma runs the kitchen, to the place I met the Tibetan trader dealing in Ghurka knives.

But here's what I loved about traveling with the sherpa: I was always free to congregate in the lodges to drink with foreign travelers, hopefully female.

The interesting thing about traveling with Mr. Canuck was the way he pushed himself, always too hard. Zoom past the pond, zoom through the village, zoom up the mountain, then bitch about the climb afterward. To smell the roses is hackneyed, but a pointless push over the mountains, going 14,000 feet up and 9,000 feet down, only to end up in the same place as everybody else, is the sign of a man that has something to prove. Mike was one of those guys, but with no other way to prove himself, he ran through the countryside like a dog biting on a rock. Yes, I'll say it again, sheer stupidity. But it put Mike in first place if anybody was keeping score on who was first.

I can race, but I much prefer meandering; pacing myself, stopping to be served tea and biscuits at 10:00 a.m. Splash the brook in my face, enjoy the countryside, contemplating the peaks. Mike and I had lots of laughs, joking back and forth with each other, sharing stories of past wives and lovers. But our friendship ended the same way they always do when climbing mountains around the world. He disappeared, never to be seen again.

"Hey Mike," I said, "Here's a picture of my girlfriend."

"Oh, yeah. A blonde! I like the way her hair shines."

"And here's one of my ex-wife."

"Oh, yeah. Very attractive. She had long brown hair, did she?

"And here's the one that got to me. Big time. Couldn't figure her out."

"Oh, yeah. She looks wicked," he said, "Sounds like she was a real bitch to you, eh?

"You've no idea. But I keep thinking about her" I said.

"Just like you keep thinking about the girl at the Lodge last night."

"Wasn't that a disappointment. I never felt so inadequate," I laughed.

"Embarrassing is what it was. I never expected it could be so small."

"I didn't either. I was thinking it was bigger in my mind. I just wanted it to grow," I said.

"No way you were going to fit her in there."

"Not with you guys laughing at it."

"It looked so pitiful, just lying there."

"Well, it was made clear, it's definitely a one-man tent."

"No shit. It's very practical, not made for love, mate."

I was with Mike when we experienced the exhilaration as we topped the last pass after Dingboche at 16,000 feet. We rounded the trail onto the glacier and there it was in all its glory. This was the first time we were in its presence. Mt. Everest, towering above all other peaks at 29,029 feet, remarkable in its height, powerful in its pyramidal form. That triangular head of granite sitting in judgement over the world. Finally, we stood before the earth's highest court. Being an attorney, I felt it had a certain judicial air.

Some people never get to see Everest because of the lousy weather. It can be socked in for weeks. To see it the first time, on a sunny day with a blue sky made the whole "expeditionary adventure" worth each step. The trek across the Himalayas for fifteen days became meaningful — thank God there's still magic in the air.

My first impression came in a soft whisper: This Mt. Everest is a bad motherfucker. Pray you will never know its wrath. It is the Man, the Paragon of Forever, the Last to Crumble. There's not a hint of fragility in its mold. Its shape is that of an oblique master. It doesn't taper to a peak, it doesn't spiral or chisel, its peak is a solid point. Mt Everest is the most secured object in Nature. What I felt was true emotion. Happiness mixed with grit. No more longing days for Everest—this is what I came for and I'll soon be part of it.

Two weeks after first seeing Everest, I had Syla take my picture in front of the Icefall at Everest Base Camp, waving goodbye. I wasn't particularly impressed with the Icefall. It's an ever-changing mountain of tumbled ice blocks as big as houses, jamming the entrance to Everest, luring you forward with crevasses that need to be crossed.

For all you hear about the danger of the Icefall you half expect it to reach out and grab you like a monster. It's supposed to be a match for the surrounding talent of mountaineers daring to be killed. But it's just another dangerous object in the way, to be analyzed and conquered.

MT. EVEREST

It's clearly not insurmountable; it just takes the cunning and guts of an extraordinarily lucky mountaineer, or the strength of a sherpa. Remember, that was Tenzing Norgay at the top of Everest with Edmund Hillary. It was Norgay in the photo because Hillary forgot to teach him how to use the camera.

I turned my back on the Icefall and Base Camp, on climbing solo to the top of Everest, on the idea of Bass helping me, and began the long trek down, which was only a bit easier than coming up. I mentioned "Periche" to my loyal expeditioners and the boys were off. I didn't see them until dark when I arrived at the village and ran into Dick Bass again, telling his same old bullshit stories. I mean, how many ways can he tell the story about Marty Hoey?

For the last time, I'll explain what happened between me and Bass. He may have paid the money for permission to climb Everest in 1983, but the real Dick never showed up. All that arrived was a fancy talker, spouting stale Texas yarns. With his head (up his ass) in a neck brace, he complained about a pinched nerve. He tried to act like he didn't know me, obviously forgetting my Birthday dinner back in Bangkok. I didn't have to remind him, he knew, but there were others to impress.

After I set the cook and water boy free, I split from Syla on the trail, something I had never done, and ended up getting lost on the upper ridge above Periche. I realized I took a wrong turn when I looked over the ridge and saw I was about 3,000 feet above the village. Try as I might, I couldn't find a trail down; and it was a sharp drop off the ridge, all the way down.

I could barely make out lights in the dusk of night. It was getting darker with only a thin sliver of moonlight. How was I going to get down, was the question? It was the first time I found myself in this predicament, and I cursed the fact it was my fault, that splitting from Syla was a bad idea. Syla, the originator of "slow, slowly!"

Of course, I had no flashlight. Why? I relied on Syla. From the time I left Gor Shep that afternoon the weather had turned bad, then turned good, bad, good, and so on. I walked through a blizzard, then heavy fog, , then falling snow, icicles clinging to my mustache and embedded in my beard. From the sizzle of the sun to the ice of the blizzard, those were the everyday conditions of climbing in the Himalayas.

Now I was stuck on a ridge with a slice of moonlight searching for a trail, any animal trail would do. I was tired after twelve hours of slogging through the elements and blamed myself for getting into this mess. Who else was I going to blame?

MT. EVEREST, NEPAL (1983)

4.

Trekking in Nepal

Trekking is a sport, filled with the drama of you struggling against nature and defying death, in your bid to become, what? It measures your ability to adapt and move on. I chose to trek 200 miles further than most, so I could say I walked from Katmandu to Mt Everest. That way I could acclimatize for my solo climb of Everest. What kind of bullshit thing is that to say? But it's true—I was in the best climbing shape of my life by the time I got to Lukla. Turns out climbing those foothills of the Himalayas work.

Lukla is where most people fly in to begin their journey up the Khumbu River. It runs towards Namche, Tengboche, Dingboche, Loboche, Periche, Gor Shep and eventually Everest. It took fifteen days of trekking paths that went straight up the mountain by design. Straight up, rather than using the less arduous switch-back design so popular in the States.

My body was not prepared for these Nepalese trails. I worked out hard, but not the right way. Running regularly at the beach and working out with weights wasn't enough. I never anticipated the stamina and strength necessary to make the motions of your body climbing stairs all day. "One leg up, next leg up."

Had I known, I'd gone to La Playa Stadium and climbed the stadium steps eight hours a day. That's the only workout that even begins to prepare you for the Himalayas. It's all in the knees, yet, the Nepalese have the skinniest legs of all.

After three days of trekking, I felt like an old fogie on the verge of going crippled. When a mountain is 11,000 feet high, your knees ache as the cartilage gets repeatedly pounded. Your full weight falls hard on your knee, and the tendons get strained when the femur crashes on your tibia, and your ligaments get strained to the max, and your meniscus gets bruised too—and you've got another 10,000 steps to go. By the time you reach the bottom, the damage is done. It's called Sahib's knee.

Metaphysics of Survival

This is the moment when you learn whether you have what it takes or not. You've got to turn yourself inside out to see what you're made of. You find out if there's any guts in there. Because if you keep going, having the guts to get there makes you feel good and you don't know why.

Trekking is tough. You'll get to a point where nothing matters anymore—wealth, spirituality, wisdom, and health go out the window. There is a power operating in the universe that makes you feel like a naturalistic mystic—riding that strain of truth that runs through universal time, the Dalai Lama's Big Book of Happiness, a certain introspective disposition that helps your energy grow. The energy that creates harmony and goodness in the universe.

Everything else is left behind. It's just you and the mountain. Every facet of your life is stripped away; the only reality is here and now. Everything's everything. What is, is?! That's both the question and the answer.

Maybe Buddha helped me realize how to survive the pain. The challenge is to put your mind at the top of the pass and climb up to it. At the top, your mind can see your body struggling in pain. But being free of the body, the mind remains impervious to it. You become your mind and leave the pain behind. There's no other way to convey the experience of trekking in the Himalayas.

As Mallory said, "It's not the ascent of the peak, but overcoming the struggle in ascending the peak."

Things weren't always in this state of ethereal transcendence. There were times I felt trekking was pointless, and I understood why somebody might not like it. Some people may think traipsing around in a full sweat by 7:00 in the morning with your legs sore is insane. At times you may feel the drudgery of lugging your load day after day, on a god forsaken journey into a devilish land, is just no fun at all. In fact, people might think it sucks, and that I was crazy.

Sometimes I would succumb to earthly demons and fall into a fit of rage. The trek would get routine, unworthy of my presence, a waste of time, and it would make me mad. Sometimes it spilled out onto the pages of my journal, some of which I will share with you:

"I'm drenched in sweat rolling in rivers over my forehead. It's a goddamn good thing I found some Ratsi in this stinking village or I was about to get pissed off. By two o'clock I hated trekking. What a miserable chore it is, nothing but up, up, up, and if it wasn't up, it's down, down, down. By four o'clock I was wishing I was someplace else—any fucking place, anything to interrupt the plot which turned me into nothing more than an endurance contest. Those fucking mountaineers must love this kind of punishment. It might be the ten-day blues, but how long can a city dweller like me enjoy the never ending up and down of these mountains?

After the 4 o'clock drudge where I was about to throw my guide and everyone else off a cliff, this path finally came to an end. And I mean finally because I was god-damn ready to call the National Guard. Thank God they had Ratsi at this village and I was able to drink away my complaints. Without that I might have been ready to kill!

I hiked better alone. Why share these joyful experiences with some jerk I'll never see again, when I can share them with all the other jerks like me who I'll be in touch with the rest of my life? Besides, this is a pilgrimage for love, money, health and metaphysics. Silence speaks best.

After the Ratsi I'm as gentle as a lamb, and I hope this picture taken by Syla of me with the lamb reflects that. But he was shaking so bad when he took the picture, you'd think he was shooting a motion picture.

This scene, the one I'm sitting in, is about as primitive as I can imagine. The cook baked pea bread in a kettle over an open fire, along with crepes and curried rice, fried potatoes, and a kettle of tea. For breakfast it was a tomato omelet with toast and jam and honey and peanut butter. Too bad for the people that follow because this whole way of life is changing. It's receding like the glaciers, and my daughter will never see it as it is today.

MT. EVEREST

The thing that irks me most is there are no women for me here, but maybe that will change too."

Forever the optimist.

The culture of Nepal is changing alright. In 2019 Nepal sold 380 Permits to climb for roughly $11,000 apiece. No doubt you've seen the photo of 320 climbers jammed in line beneath Everest's peak. All waiting their turn to complete the most extreme feat of human endurance. Waiting in line for hours at 29,000 feet in minus zero temperatures. A recipe for disaster—one person dead, seventeen for the season.

With Base Camp harboring 600 climbers at a time, it's changing and taking the entire Khumbu Valley with it. Back in 1983, Gor Shep harboured sixty-five climbers for the season. Now, it's called Gorakshep, and instead of a tiny, 5' X 10'stone outbuilding, you'll find a gigantic Super Lodge for rest and relaxation, with colorful pennants strewn about.

Lukla, where you fly in, is pretty much like Disneyland anyway. Tourists with cameras snapping pictures of cascading falls, peaks, and flowers. An old woman climbing with *two* overloaded baskets wrapped around her head. A sherpa in flip flops. It was tourism I never experienced while trekking across the fingers of the Himalayas from Katmandu.

The quaintness of Nepal has been usurped and transformed by rich, unabashed tourists. You hate to see it happen, but it was inevitable because hungry tourists eat it up—the last of a culture that has so little.

You can't help but want some as a souvenir; and suddenly, it's gone forever.

MT. EVEREST, NEPAL (1983)

5.

Everest Has a Hero

The Nepalese have cultural quirks that may be caused by ill health rather than eccentricity. But their constant coughing, hacking, and hawking phlegm on the sidewalk will certainly get your attention. It starts with some grunting, followed by a deep rumbling sound from their chest, and ends with a green gob of phlegm landing about a foot away from you. It just wasn't right.

Take a group of men standing on the corner in front of a mosque. Each is dressed smartly in robes or sports jackets. Each has their hands folded behind them and would alternate their turn to step away from the group and not so much *spit* the loogie, as to *drop* it on the sidewalk. They all do it. Hanging around a group of Nepalese is like standing next to an infirmary for heaving phlegm spatters. But nobody pays attention, or stops and says, "Hey, pal, are you okay?" They go on about their business, might drop a loogie themselves.

The children are the most entertaining. There were always children around. In the culture of Nepal the children were the only ones brave enough to say hello or even look at me. When their curiosity got the best of them, they'd sneak up and watch me writing in my journal, staring at me like it was a miracle, "White man writing in book." Syla would run them off—pesky little brats!

The cutest thing was these raggedly tag little boys in the schoolyard. They were sitting on the bench reciting their lesson in unison to their Master. They took their lessons outdoors because the one-room thatched-roof schoolhouse made-of-mud was small, and these seven boys needed sunshine. There were no girls. This was a five-day trek from Katmandu. It may as well been on the moon if you're looking for cultural evolution. The schoolyard was a tiny spec of land carved out the side of a mountain, surrounded by snowcapped peaks. You could see down the valley to our future path, zig zagging across the river.

The boys sat on their bench reading aloud, singing their lessons in harmony. Their Master, strutting back and forth, listened intently to their melody and raised his voice only occasionally upon a minor discord. I'm not sure why that was so meaningful. It made me happy to see a teacher so happy over the way his class recited their lesson.

These little boys, barefoot and in rags could travel beyond their mountain range with the confidence they could read or at least recite. The girls couldn't do that; I was sorry to see. But for the boys to read, that's not false pride, it's *real pride*. It made me think of my own daughter, six years old at the time and bigger than any of those little boys.

I can't say the same for kids around Katmandu. They seem to have an endless supply of water balloons. When I was walking in Katmandu, I kept seeing a sudden splash of water around me. Splash, there's one over there, splash, there's another one. It seemed weird, but this was Katmandu. Those crowded streets are always full of bizarre happenings.

I discovered the culprits when I took a bus ride outside of town. We saw a bunch of little brown hands caressing water balloons, standing on the side of the road, firing away at the bus.

Their favorite target is not the driver of the bus, but the conductor riding on the back taking tickets. I was next to him. But before you get the impression the bus has something akin to comfortable seating, let me be clear—there were 15 other passengers sitting and standing, crammed into and squeezed in the same three-square feet around me.

The boys loved throwing the balloons at this conductor, as though playing for a cash prize. There was no regard for safety. Did the passengers mind? Naah, the harmless free-throw of balloons at the conductor was completely acceptable child's play. The bus was speeding past the little rascals anyway, which made it fair. We were assailed every quarter mile with two-inch water balls. For fifteen miles this went on, until the bus broke down and everybody got out to fix it.

The Nepalese have no concept for lines either. When the 'coming down from Everest' portion of my adventure came to an end, I was left alone at Lukla Airport, now the Hillary Airport. Syla, the cook, and the water boy, walked back to their families at some speed. I was left at the airport to purchase a ticket for my freedom from the expedition.

It was first come, first served, at the airport, with allegedly plenty of tickets to Katmandu. But it's the Nepalese way to crowd around a closed ticket counter, rather than line up. People were pushing and shoving in a gentle fashion, but it was disconcerting and uncomfortable for anybody from a western culture. I found myself in the middle of the crowd getting pushed around, and it was still an hour until the office opened.

Behind me in the melee was an English Boy Scout Master who looked every bit the part. He was dressed in his brown uniform with the proper brocade, wearing shorts with his knee-high socks, a scarf around his neck, and he had eight Junior Scouts, ages 13–16, adorned in the same regalia.

The Master would have none of this behavior. "It's barbaric not to have a line."

He immediately began to shape up this crowd. He ordered three Scouts on each side of the crowd to begin closing ranks. The Scouts, with arms out from their side, began pressing forward in small steps to move the crowd together, forming it into a line instead of a circle. The Master and his other two Scouts worked to maintain order. The Master raising his voice to bark an order when he saw resistance, urging his Scouts to, "stand tall!".

In a matter of ten minutes there was a newly formed double line where everybody waited patiently. The Nepalese can be a very compliant bunch, but you can be certain they don't care about a "line" and would never do it again, unless coerced.

Dreams Do Come True

I thought to myself, "So this is how the Brits ruled India for all those years." First, form the Nepalese into lines, then divide them into tribes, then have the sherpas carry all your gear up the mountain. How nice of them. For myself, I got a little frustrated when I got up to the counter and couldn't buy a ticket to fly to Katmandu that day—come back tomorrow, or maybe the next day.

It's funny how things work out. Missing the plane that day was the best thing that ever happened because it allowed my dream to come true. The crown jewel on top of the crown jewel—I was going to meet Sir Edmund Hillary, the first man to summit Everest.

Missing my plane wasn't the only source of my woes that week. Syla began to think I had unlimited funds, probably because he saw me exchange cash dollars for the first time. Then, miraculously, the proprietor of the Lodge managed to charge my bill for 95 percent of whatever amount of money Syla saw me exchange that day.

I was pissed off even before I went to buy a ticket out of Lukla. But rather than go back to the Lodge and spoil my trip, I decided to hike. There was a rumor that Hillary was going to be at the Lukla School (Hillary's school for

MT. EVEREST

Sherpa) down in the Valley, about five miles away. It was suggested I go down, look at the school and, oh yes, is Ed here?

I started down the mountain trail, which was more like a dirt road, but with no cars. I stopped and got loaded on hash—something that always changes your demeanor. As I was walking casually, I was passed by a group of Sherpa children holding hands and singing as they trotted to school. They seemed to skip along without touching the ground. You'd have to have a sense for Himalayan distances to appreciate what it meant to trot to school.

This wasn't just down the street and around the corner, this was down the rugged face of a mountain, no less than 4,000 feet of vertical. The airport is at 9,000 feet. You could look down and see the school's rectangular tops. It looked like two tin roofs the size of match heads.

Off the kids scampered to school, and of course they took a short cut, zig zagging across the steep face, singing, yelling, down, down, down, they went, across the flowered paddock and through the meadows and over at least three stone fences; the only thing they didn't do was ford a river.

I followed them and it was another one of those beautiful sights I'd never seen before. If it wasn't for Edmund Hillary, there would be no school. He provided more for them than their King. The kids scarpered down the mountains together, glancing off rocks and boulders, barefoot and as agile as an Olympic athlete. They flew down the precipice as though hovering on aircushions.

MT. EVEREST, NEPAL (1983)

6.
Me and Ed Down by the Schoolyard

I got to the school yard where workers were busy chipping stone blocks and making mortar for the new building. I strolled into the yard and was first approached by a New Zealander who seemed to run the school. She was quite friendly. Upon being asked, she informed me Ed was "around here someplace."

Ed was about to take off with an assembly of older and obviously rich group of trekkers for a two- or three-day tour, depending on how Ed felt. No bones were made about that; it was all up to Ed.

"Older and obviously rich," you ask, how did I know that? Well, they were older, that's not hard to tell. I assumed these treks were provided on an "as needed basis" to raise funds for the charitable cause of gifting money to the school. That's what got Ed out of bed in the morning.

I hung around for a bit, looking the school grounds over. There were the administration, classrooms, medical building, and infirmary, but still, I couldn't find Ed. There were about twenty trekkers milling about in the yard. I looked the males over guessing: which one could be Ed Hillary?

I didn't wait around to find out. I decided to leave right then—after all, Ed was busy hobnobbing with his clients. I didn't want to bother him, nor did I want to appear the teeny-bopper-groupie hanging around to get an autograph. So, I left and became the sad sack who wouldn't allow himself to be happy. Why? I don't know. Slowly, oh so slowly, I started back up the mountain to Lukla Airport.

I was trying to figure out why I didn't try harder to meet the man. All I had to do was ask which one is Sir Edmund Hillary? Or I could have shouted his name, "Is Edmund Hillary in the house?"

How could I compare myself with the Knight, Sir Edmund? Yet, I didn't want to subject myself by acknowledging his greatness. I didn't want to proselytize myself because I was too embarrassed to act like a kid so I could meet the one man in the whole world whose autograph I wanted. What the hell was wrong with me? That's exactly what I wanted to do.

The further I got up the hill the more this made no sense. This was the chance of a lifetime. This was the man I dreamt of meeting and talking to, high in the Himalayas! Sir Edmund Hillary is a living legend, and he's here now—one of, if not my only hero! You're goddamn right I'm going down to meet him.

So back I went, and my timing was perfect. I was going to find the first lady I talked to at the clinic and ask her to point out Ed Hillary. As I was heading to the clinic all the trekkers began to move towards me. They were starting their trek now. To where? Nobody seemed to know, or care. "Just up that trail to the other side of the valley," was one trekker's response to being asked. The point of the trek wasn't where they were going, the point was they paid to have Sir Edmund Hillary lead them.

The sherpas were loaded and walking about the yard. One gent dressed in khaki shorts with a beige soft hat and a big paunch belly slowly pulled up to the lead and addressed a specific sherpa, asking if he felt okay today— it was a husky voice, deep with resonance and clear.

At the same time an attractive woman with long grey hair came up and said, "Good morning." She turned out to be Ed's daughter. I came right out and asked her which of these gentlemen approaching was Sir Edmund Hillary? He was three feet from me, the chap in the khaki shorts, coming over to talk to his daughter,

He was wide in girth but broader in the shoulders and carried a disarming smile. Old Ed had a smile as big as

Everest, with teeth like glaciers, cracked and decayed and held together with rims of gold bursting out his mouth when he smiled.

Edmund Hillary was a quiet man. Although he exuded confidence, he felt a little uncomfortable being the center of so much attention. But that's the price paid since 1953 when he first conquered Everest, and he didn't mind paying it today.

"Hi Mr. Hillary, my name is Mark Cornwall. I just had to come over here and shake hands with the man that climbed Everest," is what I said. I couldn't think of anything else.

We shook hands, and I squeezed his as hard as possible, holding it for a long time. I was excited about being in his presence and immediately proselytized myself.

"I just came from Base Camp and it is a beast of a mountain. I would never even try and summit Everest. But it gave me a real appreciation for what you accomplished," I said.

"You went all the way to base camp, did you?"

"Yeah, and I climbed Kala Patthar for the view of Mt. Everest."

"Did you get what you wanted from it?

MT. EVEREST

"I loved it, but I realize I came unprepared for the fact I'm human."

"Well, you've been as far as you can go then. You need a permit."

"I know," I said. "But I'm no Dick Bass. Ever heard of him?"

"No"

"It doesn't matter. I've come to terms with the fact I always thought I could summit Everest. Turned out I didn't really have it in me."

"You don't know that until you've had a chance to climb it."

"I had my chance and decided to pass. That honor goes to someone way more committed than I," I said.

"Committed to what? There's more to life than climbing Mt. Everest. But it took me twenty years to find what the "more to life" was. And it was right in front of me. Look around you! What do you see everywhere in the Khumbu Valley? Little scruffy children with no place to get an education. What lies in their future, but more of the same? I'm trying, my family, everybody here is trying to help them get educated. For the last ten years we've been trying."

"Wow, now there's a commitment," I said, "How's that make you feel. Like you're on top of the world?"

"Better than that. The last time I was there it was a mite bit freezing, mate."

I laughed and wondered where I'd be in ten years. Then I pulled a Robert Ludlum novel out of my back pocket.

"Would you please sign the back of my book. I've never asked anybody for their autograph before," I said with a shy smile.

That got a knee slap from his daughter. It was fun for her to see her father adored in such a venerable way. Everybody was happy, and I most of all.

I looked Ed straight in his eyes, but they eluded me. They were hiding deep in his sockets. How did the man ever get up Everest with eyes that deep? Or did that condition come about after Everest? When he suddenly faced the world in his greatness, did his eyes then retreat so his soul didn't get stolen?

We shook hands twice after he wrote on the last page of my book, his name, "Ed Hillary." I asked him about it, "No Sir Edmund?" and he said, "Just call me Ed."

Ed was 63 years old at that time and went on to provide educational benefits for the Sherpa another 23 years until his death at age 88. In my opinion, no greater man has walked the earth.

    I found my way down from the ridge above Periche when a path mystically appeared before me. It wasn't a real path you could see and follow; it was more a trail left by a run of field mice, made visible only by deposits of food droppings no bigger than a pellet. The trail wound from the top of the ridge to the back door of the lodge. Somewhat unbelievable, I know. But it led me thousands of feet down to the warm glow of the fire, and Syla pacing around outdoors waiting for me.

    The next morning the bunion on my right foot was so swollen and painful I couldn't get my boot on. But get it on I must. There's no calling in sick or lying in bed for days until the swelling goes down. I've got to go now. I'm not letting Mike Dunlop get ahead of me.

The autograph of Sir Edmund Hillary

MT. EVEREST

The yak kicking my ass   Ratsi and my lil' lamb

The cook and waterboy   Syla, my guide
making pea bread

MT. DENALI, ALASKA (1988)
7.
Motivation for Climbing Denali

Have you ever wondered what it's like to climb the highest mountain in Alaska? I had the pleasure of climbing Denali in 1988 with Vern Tejas, the first to summit Denali solo, in winter of that same year; and Art Davidson, a participant in the trio that first summited Denali in the winter of 1967.To commemorate their success, they decided to have a 20-year reunion by climbing Denali with invited guests. And I was one.

I rang Alaska Travel sometime in April 1988, to set up a tour guide to climb Denali, (It was Mt. Mckinley at the time, and technically is again, though most climbers and natives have always just called it Denali) and they hooked me up with the outfitters supplying Vern and Art's team leaving the first week of August—a very late date to start.

I was delighted when Mt. McKinley changed its name to Denali. It was about time. It's located in Denali National Park, on the Denali Preserve, surrounded by 6,000,000 acres of Denali Forest full of deciduous taiga, alpine tundra, glaciers, and snowy mountains. Why not name it Denali, given that's its native namesake? There was a time in the summer of 1988, when Mt. McKinley drew the attention of mountain lovers everywhere to the ensemble of "wannabe" mountaineers, or "client adventurers" as Vern likes to call them. Vern Tejas won the hearts of his fellow Alaskans by becoming the first to step foot on the 20,310-foot peak, solo, in the middle of that same winter of 1988.

Also assembling for the climb was Art Davidson, the other climber to step on the summit of North America's highest peak in the middle of winter, twenty years earlier. This 44-year-old was a member of that team effort to make the first and only other winter ascent on February 28, 1967. The other two members of his trio were Dave Johnston and Ray Genet. Art was 21 years old at the time and wrote a book about the climb, precociously named: *Minus 148 Degrees*.

You'd think a man who wrote a book at 21 about surviving six days above 18,000 feet in temperatures so low it registered Minus 148 degrees with the wind chill would have climbed a little further up the adventure ladder. But Mt. McKinley was his oyster, and the mountains were his sea.

Art's partner, Ray "Pirate" Genet, became the *esprit* of Alaska's mountaineering world. He was the godfather of Alaskan outfitters, coining the phrase, "To the Summit." He died of hypothermia at 28,000 feet on Mt. Everest, October 2, 1979. I'm not saying Davidson should have followed Genet's example and perished on Everest, but it seems odd that Art just quit. There might be a story there.

Dave Johnston went on to be the first climber to accomplish winter ascents of the highest peaks in all fifty states. He climbed them all in the summer too. And if you think a winter ascent of Mt. Rainier would be easy, ask Mr. Johnston about his third try.

Davidson returned to Denali twenty years later to celebrate the twentieth anniversary of his bold winter ascent of McKinley in 1967, sharing it with the only other person who climbed solo in the winter of 1988. Also on the climb was Art's 18-year-old son named Dylan Davidson. Never far from Dylan's lips was the sound of Bob Marley singing, "We be jammin…" Like father, like son. They were both tall and slender. But there was something missing from both, and I was darned if I couldn't figure it out.

It had been five years since I was last in the mountains. I was never part of a climbing "team," but being 38 years old at the time, I figured there was no other way I could get to the summit. All I had to do is whatever Vern Tejas told me to do. Placing my trust in the right person meant making it to the top. And once I met Vern, I had no doubt that I was trusting the right man.

We met up in Talkeetna. I remember going through a gear check when it came out that I was an attorney. I might as well have said I had impetigo. Ace and Jennifer Lane, the husband-and-wife team that joined us seemed like a nice couple. He was a professional downhill skier, and she was his trainer. She was by far in the best shape of anybody on the team, but they both were into numerology.

They kept writing numbers in the snow that were supposed to mean something, and they would giggle about it, but it was all a big secret they kept to themselves. We were about eight days out and getting ready to make camp at 14,500 when the numbers went bad.

Vern kindly let them use the sat-phone so they could check with their spiritual guide—which was very important to them. The numbers were not in their favor. After much thought, the couple decided to quit the team and head back to the Kahiltna International Airport to catch a ride home. No refunds. No shit.

There were two other paying customers. Christian was from Austria but spoke English better than most of us, which was good because he was talkative. His culture and sarcastic wit made him a candidate for best friend on the team, and garnered lots of laughs. At least I was laughing. We shared the same tent for 16 nights, until our camp at 17,500 feet, when I got switched to Art and Dylan's tent.

Christian and I got along so well that I hated making the switch. I thought for sure we'd get together and party in Vienna afterward. But when I wrote to him, telling of my plan to come to Europe and visit him in Austria, he never wrote me back. Just another one-time climbing partner, but a fun one.

Then there was Nancy. I tried my hardest not to get stuck in her tent and was successful. Not unattractive, I thought she might need more than I could give. She spent her tent time with Art and Dylan, until 17,500 when she got switched to Christian and Buck's tent, the assistant guide on the trip. But I think most of her waking hours were spent with me. She always placed herself next to me on the rope, and as best I remember, she was always within close earshot. But then, the camps were small, so everyone else was within earshot too. There was no getting away from somebody.

Our group traveled from Talkeetna to the Kahiltna Glacier via snow plane. There's plenty of room on the

MT. DENALI

glacier for landing and taking off. You can move your camp a little further north where there's more room for dividing up food, loading your sled, and weeding through the gear you'll want to stash.

You'll want to pay close attention when your guide shows you how to save your partner if he's sliding over the edge of a crevasse by arresting his fall. That's information you can use. We spent an entire day putting over-boots on our plastic boots, showing off our glasses, sharing our gear, strutting our new threads and looking at the full-frontal view of the "Great One." Looking big, Denali! It was a grand blue sky. All you can see is blue above and white below. No trees in sight.

Buck told me about a would-be climber who came out, took one look at the monster mountain looming above, turned around and caught the next plane back. I patted my pocket to make sure I had my glasses, then remembered they were on my head. That would be the stupidest mistake you could make, forgetting your sunglasses. I was reminded by a guy begging for glasses, "Hey, hey, any of you guys got a pair of extra glasses?" His only other option would be to go snowblind due to excessive ultra-violet radiation from the sun reflecting off the snow and ice. Nobody had an *extra* pair.

Yes, you must pull a sled full of food, fuel, stoves, pots and pans. You put on your full expedition pack, strap a lariat around your waste and attach it to the sled. It's probably 70+ pounds, not really a problem because your pace is slow. You're roped up to a three-or four-man rope, with 30 feet of rope between each of you. If one of you should fall into a crevasse, the person in front or behind you should have time to react and catch your fall.

There will always be 30 feet between you, as the group is climbing single file up the mountain. When you stop climbing, it will be for lunch or because you have arrived at a point where you're making camp. You're not walking around. The perimeter of the camp, which includes the latrine, will be outlined for you, and you are never going beyond those lines—beyond those lines the guides cannot say if there is a crevasse or not.

This is not a mountain you are free to roam around on. It should not be your choice if you like long walks after dinner, you like being alone, or you'd just like to explore the other side of the mountain. This is not that type of mountain. You will stay with the group inside those lines, and you will enjoy the mountain from there. Yes, you will also piss and shit inside those lines.

MT. DENALI

It was the beginning of August, and we were off to a late start. In fact, we were the last guided party of the season. That meant conditions were getting wet and sloppy, making a bigger threat of avalanches, snow bridges collapsing, and crevasses widening. Plus, it was getting hotter. The first ten days of the climb were in the 90's. We'd strip down to nothing, bare skin, hydrating as best we could. We made our way slowly across the ice and snow to reach 14,500 feet in ten days.

But we weren't in any rush. We weren't climbing Alpine style—light and fast. We were performing the "siege technique" of expedition climbing and making absolutely sure each person was acclimatized to make the summit. We didn't have rest days, but we had days in which we lugged a load of gear to the next camp and came back to our current camp to sleep. We'd carry a load to 11,000 feet, come back to sleep at 9,500; hump a load up to 14,500; come back and sleep at 11,000; ferry to 16,000; back to 14,500. You get it. With the hours of light in a day being somewhere around twenty, it began to feel like just one long day—until it wasn't.

The Climb Begins

We started off from Kahiltna International Airport. The name identifies the packed snow landing strip at the end of the Kahiltna Glacier that is a climber's entryway to the West Buttress of Denali and receives climber from every corner of the globe. We were one happy bunch of campers with our packs and sleds overflowing with goodies.

"Hey, you want to take *War and Peace*; why not, we're taking all the rest of the crap," seemed to be our ethos.

We took off in the afternoon, heading straight up the glacier to a camp about 7,800 feet. That's not a typo—that's as much elevation as you get starting off. It's slow but not arduous. Just nine people on three ropes, walking end to end up a glacier.

We passed a Spaniard who was climbing solo. Three attempts were made to communicate with him in Spanish. One of them was me, and we all decided he must be from the far north because we couldn't understand a word he said. All the previous crevasse flags had been blown down, so Vern dutifully put up new ones to mark dangers. And before you knew it, we were at our first camp.

MT. DENALI

But I didn't feel so good. I broke out in a cold sweat. Trying to look like I was okay, I asked a couple of people how they felt. Great, they alleged, as they started to shore up the perimeter wall, build the latrine, set up the tents, get out the cooking gear, make some tea, and sort everything out. Then, *ka-thunk*—my heart went out of sinus rhythm. It felt like my heart was going to flutter away and die. All I wanted to do was take a break and watch the others build a fort. Atrial fibrillation could not have been more unwelcome.

I tried not to miss a beat. I grabbed the ice saw to cut bricks and help wall up the perimeter from wind, an impossible job as I later realized. Then, I used the shovel to shape some seats out of snow so we could sit. I swept a nice flat pad to rest the tent on and made several trips for clean snow to melt for water. I didn't say a word.

The whole time I knew what my problem was. I knew what it had been for the last decade. It was dissipation. It was all those drinks I had consumed and all those all-nighters I had pulled since climbing the Himalayas just five years ago. I shuddered at the thought. But that was the reason I was on this climb.

A Reason to Climb

I was at home in Summerland, California when I made the decision. It was April of 1988, and I had two things on my mind. First, I wanted to get as far away as possible from a girl named Gilda. I'd been unhappy for a long time. Gilda loved me but was driving me crazy with her version of love. I loved her too, or pretended to. And I allowed her to manipulate me in a way I enjoyed, a repulsive way to love each other. I was supposed to be happy, but I wasn't feeling happy. She said she made me happy, that I would miss the shit out of her if she was gone, and I would have. But that didn't mean she made me happy. I'd be able to tell if I was experiencing happiness, wouldn't I?

Secondly, nobody just gets up one morning and starts their adventure of climbing the seven summits. For most people, it's a long story of preparation. I lived in Alaska between the ages of 24 and 27, and I never dreamed of climbing Denali. I heard of people that did, and I thought they were crazy. Have you any idea how difficult, how cold and how dangerous that can be?

Ten years later, I'm trying to summit the monster. Why did I throw caution to the wind and choose the

MT. DENALI

absolute most uncomfortable and perilous summer vacation possible, let alone take on the challenge of mountain climbing on ice 20,310 feet in the Arctic? What made me suddenly think I could do that, and how could I possibly think that could be fun? And why?

The answer is, I was bored to death. Do not underestimate the power of your office chair to cripple you before it kills you. As you're being crippled, the chair works on your mind. You start thinking you are an old man, condemned to the fate of that chair. Worse, you're no longer a man. You are a fattening shadow of who you think you are. You're dying of stress, with a drinking problem, and you're only 38 years old. You know what I mean if when you're walking downtown, you glance up and catch a view of a person in the big plate glass window, who you don't know. That can't be you, not the guy with the belly?

I came back to the office with my cup of coffee and called Alaska Travel who hooked me up with the Ray Genet outfitters. They told me they added one last expedition beginning at the end of July. That gave me three months to get in shape. My timing was impeccable.

My heart palpitations were gone, never to visit me again during this fateful climb. I was sleeping when my heart caught a beat to put it back in sinus rhythm. And that's where it remained for the length of this trip. Working loads daily, my heart was steady as a rock. But I always had the fear of it going out of rhythm right when I needed it most.

We were six days out by the time we camped at 11,000 feet. That's only 2,000 feet higher than our first night out. They were sunny days, every one of them. Our location on the mountain didn't reveal much landscape because we were climbing in the Kahiltna Valley. We had to work our way up the valley and around the ridge at Windy Corner, to establish our base camp on the plateau at 14,500 feet.

From the 11,000-foot camp to our new base camp at 14,500, it was 3,500 vertical feet. This was the first real challenge for all of us, except for maybe Jennifer, who was dancing circles around Ace. I was humored how every time she did that, he'd start scribbling numbers in the snow with his ski pole. I wondered if her frolicking in the snow bridled him in some way; but I was struggling so hard for my own breath, I couldn't make sense of it.

We carried only light gear such as extra fuel, groceries, cold weather gear, and the like, dropping it off at Windy Corner, then returning to sleep at our 11,000-foot camp. The next morning, we were rewarded for our brutal effort by taking a full day to play around the camp. Something the Alpinist never does because he's in a rush.

Cultural Delay

This day of lollygagging at 11,000 feet was eventually rewarded by a $250 gratification check paid for by the *Anchorage Times*.

The six of us "wannabe" climbers felt honored to climb in the company of Vern Tejas and Art Davidson. These were two heroes recorded in the annals of mountaineering for making their individual winter ascents of Denali, and we were proud to be on the team. There was plenty of press in Alaska interested in the story of this quasi-historic event. To that end, the *Anchorage Times* asked for any photographs we may want to share with their readers — anything from a snow leopard to a line of fatigued climbers.

I picked out about ten photos I thought might make the grade. But then I thought, who am I to judge what makes a picture better than everyone else's? So I bundled up the whole pack, negatives and all, and shoved them in an envelope to the *Times* and hoped for the best. I hoped they would publish one because that's the only way the photo could be seen.

I was surprised at the one they chose. It was a picture of a mountain taken through a block of ice, while sitting in the latrine. As we were kicking around camp, with all the time in the world, I decided to head to the latrine to think things over. It was another sunny afternoon. The latrine was built sturdily on the south-east side of the camp. It was the second day of absorbing 90-degree heat, so the integrity of the latrine began to break down. That meant the sun was beginning to penetrate the middle of our three-foot-high privacy wall.

Each block of ice was stacked one upon the other, dripping from top to bottom, looking like crystal sunshine inside. Shiny white on top, each block gradually melted down to a clear spot in the center. A tiny hole in the center of the brick showed a mountain on the other side, framed by the opaque rivulets running down the brick. Because the ice was melting, the photo of the mountain through the pinhole in the frozen block appeared to be a brilliant study in contrast; or so I guessed.

That was the one chosen and printed in black and white. It made you feel like you were sitting next to an ice boulder staring at a snowcapped mountain through ice clouds. The *Times* didn't know I was sitting on the throne at the time. I wonder if it would have made a difference.

In reality, our camp was pitched next to a massive slab of ice so high you couldn't see the top of it. We were still on the upper Kahiltna Glacier. Completely dwarfed like little pinnacles against the wall. Nobody was in front of us, and nobody behind us either. We wondered what happened to the Spaniard. There was no trace of him.

No, we were all alone. Questions were beginning to arise regarding the speed of our climb, but nothing out loud. We had plenty of food, no one was hurt, and all was at peace. In the morning we'd climb beyond Windy Corner to make base camp at 14,500.

Problems at Windy Corner

We moved from the Kahiltna campsite up to our 14,500-foot camp on the ninth day, a Monday. On Tuesday we established basecamp, then ventured back to Windy Corner and returned with the rest of our gear. On Wednesday, we moved food and supplies up to 16,000 feet, then returned to basecamp to sleep. Gale force winds kept us huddled in our tents for Thursday, Friday, and Saturday.

Six more days had passed, and we weren't any closer to the summit than we were on Monday. We were still in basecamp. The breakdown of August 9th through 14th, reads as follows:

<u>Monday</u>: After sunning ourselves on the rest day, we were eager to get off the glacier and onto the massif to begin "real" climbing. The Kahiltna Glacier ends on a wide plateau across the mountain, giving us our first panoramic view of the surrounding landscape. There was static in the air that a fundamental difference was coming to the expedition—Ace and Jennifer were going to quit the climb.

We ate lunch at Windy Corner where you could see over the tops of mountains for miles. Mt. Foraker was right in front of us. Vern told us on his previous climb, he could barely stand up right where he stood now because of the wind. It wasn't like that for us. We ate our pre-made sandwiches and candy bars, drank our lemonade and listened to a barely audible undercurrent of fear coming from Jen and Ace. If not fear, then an uneasy feeling that something wasn't quite right.

Jennifer was a friendly girl, very attractive in a cute way, and madly in love with Ace, her big downhill skiing husband. Being his trainer was obviously demanding, but she did a great job of motivating him. So what was the problem?

Neither she nor Ace were saying. They kept it to themselves. They played this game of writing numbers in the snow to each other as we marched in single file. The numbers could have been biblical scriptures or a spiritual message from outer space, but they weren't sharing. It was all hush, hush. If she was in front of him on the rope, she would write symbols in the snow, like "#NL69" with her ski pole. He'd come along, look at the numbers, laugh then erase it so the person behind him couldn't see it. And he'd do the same. But they weren't laughing now.

They never offered an explanation. They'd talk about anything but that. But something was gnawing at them. By the time we finished lunch at Windy Corner the grumbling grew louder and was now being heard by the rest of us. The two of them alone with Vern on that first rope gave them the opportunity to discuss their conundrum in private with Vern.

The problem was: the numbers weren't coming up right, although we could never figure where they came from in the first place. In fact, they must have come up horribly wrong. They must have been saying, "Don't go on; stop this insanity, or you will be killed. If you go further, the gods will raise their ugly heads against you. You'll get dropped into a crevasse, or you'll fall climbing the headwall and roll into a giant snowball as you fall back to the Kahiltna International Airport. What are you thinking stupid? Go back! Get outta here!"

Jennifer and Ace conferred more with Vern over their grave issue. Vern took the subject very seriously and allowed them to call their spiritual leader on the sat phone for proper advisement. He obviously grasped the multitude of various deadly scenarios all leading back to him.

This is what was at stake. They spent $14,000 to fly to Alaska for the greatest adventure of their lives. They also paid a premium to get top notch gear, such as boots, sleeping bags, and cold weather gear that's very expensive, times two. They were in terrific shape having spent hundreds of hours on physical training. But time always comes at a price. They had been on the climb ten days, so half the struggle was over for God's sake. Only the most dangerous part of the climb was left. There were no obvious problems. All they had to do was put one foot in front of the other and follow Vern up the mountain.

As soon as we got to 14,500 feet, I grabbed a shovel and headed over to dig out the new latrine. My fate had been set; I was making this latrine the granddaddy of them all. But as I was digging and scraping the new outhouse, looks of despair bounced back and forth between the worried couple as they sought more advice.

<u>Tuesday</u>: The last thing I heard Ace mumble, as he shuffled out of camp was, "Well, there goes $14,000 bucks."

Vern escorted Ace and Jennifer back to Kahiltna International to catch their ride home. What got into them? It was the 1,500 feet of headwall we could now see and were going to climb in a couple of days. It's one heck of a headwall, taking us to the 16,000-foot mark. I was looking forward to it. I had been to 16,000 feet once before in Nepal and was eager to meet the challenge. Besides that, there were fixed ropes to latch onto—what more could we ask for?

But now Vern wouldn't be back for a day, maybe two. So, we descended to pick up the last remaining gear we had cached at Windy Corner. Then we fortified the basecamp with thicker ice walls to protect us from wind, ate, and relaxed for the rest of the day.

<u>Wednesday</u>: This was the best day on ice ever! We spent the morning climbing the headwall, lugging supplies up to the 16,000-foot camp. That part was filled with sweat from pulling our sleds straight up the mountain using the fixed line. Our path was crisp and hard because it hadn't

snowed for at least two weeks, so there were no steps to cut into the ice. The path was packed snow, which our crampons gripped easily, and made the path practically lift us up the grade. It was a matter of step, apply the muscle, and step again. Conditions ideal.

The fun came when we descended. Looking down from 16,000 feet was unbelievably steep. It was treacherous, and fun. At the bottom, where the fixed rope was attached, the ice wall fans out across the mountain's plateau, into a long, wide landing pad, before it drops off again. No matter how fast you went down the hill, you couldn't fly off the mountain. There was 1,000 feet—over three football fields—of unobstructed downhill sledding. You put your pack on the sled, lay down on your pack, and point the sled towards Base Camp. Whoosh! You were on the most glorious sled ride of your life, on the most perfectly contoured sledding hill in America. What a blast!

<u>Thursday, Friday and Saturday.</u> Blizzard conditions.

"Well, this sucks." (Quote from journal, Saturday, August 14, 1988)

MT. DENALI, ALASKA (1988)

8.

"To the Summit!"

The blizzard came slowly, starting with a gust and building continuously. Before long it turned into an angry god, slapping us with the wind, not caring if tent stakes were pulled up and thrown at your face. It mutated into an ugly snowstorm, then a maelstrom using snowflakes as missiles, before deciding to dump as much snow on us as possible. First heavily, then lightly, until it was all gone and not a single snowflake was left to crown the earth.

Inside our tent we relaxed across each other, head to toe, four, maybe five to a three-man tent. Boots were off, either left covered outside or impeccably cleaned off inside. There was Art Davidson on the inside grimacing every time somebody came in. As soon as the flap opened came the cry, "Don't let any snow in goddamit. You're letting snow in."

He had good reason, I guess. Any snow was like throwing a hand full of ice in the tent. It would warm up, melt on the bags, freeze at night, and then you've got ice in your bag forever. That's how Art treated one flake, so you can imagine how a freezing camper sticking his head in our tent for a friendly "hello," snowflakes falling from their grinning face, might get an uncomfortable greeting such as, "Get those fucking flakes out of here!"

When the blizzard quit after four days, we were left in a wonderland of fresh fallen snow, three feet of it. It was beautiful, like seeing the mountain for the first time. There wasn't a footprint to be seen, pure white all the way up to the head wall and beyond. But what was pleasant to the eyes was a nightmare to climb. A goddam fucking nightmare.

It was time to get ready for the cold, which meant pulling out all the stops as far as dress goes. Starting with long underwear, I put on three types: tight ones, the kind you normally wear, and the extra heavy. I wore a pair of Patagonia fleece pants that had zippers down both sides, and Patagonia bib overalls with suspenders to keep me dry. Up top I wore the same three layers of blue Patagonia long undershirts, a green fleece jacket, a red windbreaker, and a grey GORE-TEX overcoat. (All on sale at the Patagonia rack.)

For my hands, I had liners, gloves, wool mittens, and blue over-mittens. It's safe to say I had no problems with the cold; it's stripping everything off that's a problem.

MT. DENALI

Taking a dump was a chore. For that reason, I went twenty-one days without changing my underwear and twenty-one days without brushing my teeth. I don't have an excuse for not brushing my teeth, except it was too much trouble.

Dressed to kill, I was ready for the headwall with no idea what we were facing. I can't speak for everyone, but I saw no happy faces when we reached the headwall. We were lucky to get started at all, with Vern so upset over the conditions. We moved slowly out of basecamp towards the fixed ropes only two hundred yards away. That distance across the plateau in three feet of new snow was nerve racking. It meant with every step you took, you slung your leg around and it sunk a foot, before lugging the other leg around again. Our bobsled run was giving us serious problems, but we survived in good shape until we hit the headwall.

We were somewhere around the fixed rope area, but it's hard to say. Last time we were there the fixed rope was open and obvious, waiting to latch onto and go. Now you couldn't see the rope anywhere. It was somewhere, but three feet of snow was covering it up. The rope may be 50 feet to the right or left, over there, or…over there. No, wait. Vern went to work as best he could, diving headfirst in the snow trying to find the rope. Not an easy job, but it was his.

It wasn't hard on us, standing around, waiting waste deep in snow for him to say, "Voila, I've found it." But an hour passed, and it wasn't found.

Vern would move over ten, twenty, thirty feet, and each time he'd dive down and come up with nothing. He'd move up and back. We ate lunch and ruminated on the subject; nobody had an idea. Vern was getting mad. He wasn't a guy who cursed, but you could hear him say "shit" and then a louder "fuck." The possibility of our ascent being delayed was disheartening, but not as disheartening as after the third hour when the words came you never thought you'd hear: "I quit."

None of us knew what to do. Buck said he'd try the other side, it's okay, take a break. Vern was about forty feet from me, burning amber. He was chest deep in snow, and if he said it was the end, it was. He stood there in a cataclysmic trance. Then, making a last effort beyond all hope, he buried his head in the snow and dove to depths unknown to come up with, "Voila, I found it!"

We were in business again. We roped in and I was fourth in a line of seven. The idea behind a fixed rope is to help you get up a 45 percent slope without the risk of falling off and being lost to the abyss. The fixed rope was really four ropes, eighty meters long, anchored to the side

MT. DENALI

of the mountain, and strung end to end to cover 1,000 feet, bottom to top.

As you approach the rope, you hook onto it with an ascender. The ascender is a metal clamp that attaches to the fixed rope and automatically tightens when weight is applied and relaxes when weight is removed. The ascender is attached to you with a 36-inch tie that wraps through your climbing harness, so you don't lose it. The ascender's purpose is to hold you to the mountain so you won't fall off.

But in 1988, there was no automatic ascender, another contrivance not yet invented. You had to squeeze the metal ascender open and keep squeezing it, if you wanted to climb up, sliding it up an arm's length of fixed rope, while taking a step, using the ascender for balance, then taking a step with the other leg. Squeeze and repeat again. You're fixed to the rope, so you don't have to worry about falling. But you've got to keep sliding the ascender up the rope, one stroke after the other, in unison with the person in front of and behind you.

Imagine.

This takes a lot of coordination when climbing a headwall. But it's even more important to keep in time with the other climbers. You're tied into the line and have a 60-pound pack on your back. There is three feet of snow, and you are pulling a sled. Climbing a 45 percent slope is tough enough, but it's a 1,000-foot climb with six other climbers, and no breaks.

The problem is everybody has different climbing speeds and gaits. If you could put your foot in the footprint of the person in front of you it would be much easier, so you try. But then the snow bulks up, or you step into a hole that swallows your whole leg, you lose your grip on the jumar, or your ice axe gets caught in the apparatus. There are lots of things that can go wrong, and you don't want to hold up the train.

I was behind Dylan Davidson. He was climbing the way you would expect an 18-year-old to climb: fast and frenetic. We were both tall so all I had to do was follow in his footsteps, jumar in one hand, ice axe in the other. We were plunging away, me doing everything possible to keep up the pace, concentrating on my breath. I hyperventilated four times between each step, then five times. That's heavy breathing.

I looked up and saw the reddish, sharp stones jetting out from the ridge, just ahead of us. It was the beginning of the West Buttress, and the spot of our makeshift camp for the night. The ridge was about thirty feet wide on top, then fell off the other side 3,000 feet—but there's a natural rock barrier that keeps you safe.

    I saw Vern go over the top of the crest and disappear. That left only Art, Dylan, and me, with Nancy, Christian and Buck following behind, one every fifteen yards. I was almost too tired to think about it at the time, but it looked like I might be the guy in the worst shape. I wasn't in bad shape, but I mean, take Nancy for example. I looked at her beet-red face, contorted into agony, begging to get this wall behind her. She smiled at me, loving it. I smiled back.

Wonders Never Cease

    Something happened to Art Davidson that next morning. Something inspired him to prove he was part of that first group to summit Denali in winter 1967. He asked Vern if he could go first on the rope, along the ridge route that skirts up the edge of the cliff, leaving no room for error.

    He was always second to Vern anyway, so it was no big deal. The team needed Vern down the line where Christian was having problems climbing over the icecap. Dylan was getting impatient, and Nancy was sure Christian was going to pull her into the basin far below.

Christian was a very truthful mountaineer, never acted like he could over-climb a dangerous situation, and in this case the situation was dangerous, so he was taking his time. It was necessary to kick steps in the ice to get your crampons to grab onto the block instead of skimming across the top. You were guarded by an outlying crop of rocks to the left, but to the right was only two feet before it dropped off the rock precipice, showing nothing but sharp protrusions all the way down.

Christian was kicking the ice and cleaning it with his ice axe, his huge pack weighing him down. He was in a crouching position when his leg got the sewing-machine twitch, quivering like a vibrator. It's an involuntary reaction, a force of nerves happening in your leg. But when you see it, it makes others get nervous because they're in the same vulnerable spot.

I took the opportunity to watch Art. He was moving gracefully as though on skis; in a manner I'd never seen in him. To hell with being held back, he was off-leash and powering with each stride over any obstacle in his way. His head was up; his gait was long. He'd disappear around a nodule and come right back around the corner. I don't know if he knew where he was going, but between 16,000 and 17,000 feet, he was getting there fast.

MT. DENALI

It reminded me of a horse. You rent them for an hour; and for forty-five minutes you're cursing and prodding them to go. Then, the minute you turn for home it's Katie bar the door. They start running as fast as they can, until they can't run anymore. They slow down to a gallop, then a trot, and by the time you get them back to the barn, they are worked up into a foaming sweat and can't breathe. They just plod in. Then the stable master gets so spitting mad he goes apoplexy and says you're going to give his horse pneumonia. That's the way Art Davidson just took off.

We didn't catch up with him for a couple of hours. But that night we were sharing the same tent, so I asked what had gotten into him. Dylan was there too, all snuggled cozy like in our three-man tent. Art and I with our heads at one end and Dylan at the other, when I asked, "It's like you were breaking for the barn, there was no stopping you."

Dylan said, "Yeah, the barn door was wide open, and you were going for it?"

Art, somewhere deep in his sleeping bag, never answered us. He just lay there in silence. Such was the personality of Art Davidson. I never could figure him out.

We caught up with Art at the 17,500 camp. I was excited because being in the "last" camp is what this endeavor's all about. But Vern had one more surprise for us. He said, "I want Nancy and Christian to stay here and make camp. You four come with me. We're going back to the 16,000-foot camp to retrieve the remainder of the supplies".

Say again?

Vern made the instructions very clear. Yes, we had done a full day's work, but the weather was perfect, it may go bad tomorrow, and there is no time to delay. "We need those supplies. Nancy, Christian stay; the rest of you, come with me."

So backward we marched, making good time on the way down. When we got there, Vern and Buck divided the supplies between us, giving us enough food for a week. This is the spot where Vern randomly asked me if everything was okay. I answered, "My heart feels like it's going to explode, and if it does there's going to be a big mess, blood everywhere, splattering all over the snow," animating my arms for effect.

Vern looked at me and said, "Okay, then let's go!"

I can't remember squat about the climb back; except we made good time. I do remember what happened after we got there because we hadn't expected it. Vern got angry.

MT. DENALI

He got really mad at Nancy and Christian for sitting around on their lazy asses doing nothing.

I suppose in Vern's mind he saw this duo going right to work, setting up camp, putting up the tents, separating the gear ascribed to each tent, building a latrine, preparing a kitchen; hell, they had enough time to do all off that and put on a kettle of water, so we could have tea. I'll bet he was thinking we'd be drinking tea.

Instead, what he saw was two people sitting around like they were on vacation. Truth be known, they probably sat down on their packs, and the whole world slowed down with them. With nobody else there, it's hard to say if it's been five minutes or ten or thirty. The view was spectacular. The cloud layer had lifted long ago; it was the American "frontier" down there. Beyond that was nothing but snowcapped peaks and glaciers, with green tundra for miles—600,000,000 acres of it. This is Alaska, and one thing about Alaska is its border is huge.

Nowhere in the world have six men and a woman humped so much gear over such hostile and exposed terrain. On the other side of the West Buttress is the view of the Autobahn, and the trail leading above it is to Denali Pass. Beyond that is the unknown stairway to the stars, the mystery of the universe. It goes 3,000 feet higher leading us to Summit Ridge, then across the Football Field to the summit. Tell me you couldn't just stare at that for hours, dreaming of where you've been and where you're going to go. If only you were left undisturbed. C'mon man!

It was Vern's failure to communicate specifically what needed to be done. Maybe Nancy heard Vern tell her, "Take a break, you've been working too hard." As it was, it's a four-hour tour to 16,000 feet and back, so there was no excuse. And there was nothing we could do but dig in and build a camp. I was too tired to be pissed. It was fun enough to hear Vern's outrage about it, and then, because we only had two tents, Vern volunteered to sleep outside. I don't know what he was thinking because it gets mighty cold outside at 17,500 feet.

The next day was a rest day. I couldn't believe it; we were so close, and it was a perfect day. It may be our only chance. But we got up late and lazed around, ate breakfast, then returned to our bunks and rested all day.

There are precautions to consider. At 17,500 feet, we're in the death zone; our bodies are wearing down faster than they are building up and will continue to do so. As much trouble as we went through to acclimatize, we were not immune to the subtleties of hypoxia. We could starve for oxygen if given enough time. But that's the beauty of the 'siege technique.' We had worked and paid for our time. We were seventeen days on the mountain, and none of us had any signs of acute mountain sickness. We were in good shape, and it was relaxing to have the extra day. We'd be ready the next morning.

    Summit Day had finally come, and it was sunny again. The first thing we ate was a bowl of Lucky Charms. I liked the poetic touch but thought it lacked the nourishment to last what was to be a very long day. But I didn't voice my concern because I was dwelling on the job at hand. There's no way of knowing what to expect. I'd never been at that elevation. What was it like at 18,000 or19,000 and so on? What about the weather? It can change at any moment. What will it be like, eight or ten hours from now?

    Questions. Too many questions about our future. I really didn't care. I just wanted to get moving. Now. If a storm came up and blew us off the mountain, so be it. We're here so let's make the most of it for as long as we can. And I pray to God I have the strength to...Shit, I know I have the strength. Let's go!

Crossing the Autobahn

The Autobahn was so named because if you slipped on the ice, you'd be like a Kraut pushing the accelerator to the floorboard of his BMW, picking up more speed as you swooshed down the mountain, and vanished into the abyss at the bottom, like going down into the toilet. The Autobahn is a monolithic plane of ice covering the entire east side of the West Buttress. It spreads from our camp in the West to the other side of the mountain at Denali Pass in the East.

The trail to Denali Pass starts at the south end of the Autobahn. It heads straight for the Pass, following a gradient of 10% for a mile or more in length. It's one of the most memorable parts of the climb.

The ice mass you're walking on stretches up to your right, and slants down to your left. It stretches for a mile, and when you look down you see how the ice swirls around for some 3,000 feet, until it flattens out into a hole. The trail is precarious because you only have a single file path to walk on. You can't go left or right. I you did fall, your climbing partners could watch you slide down until poof—you're gone.

As we started out it was slow going. Vern blazed the trail, kicking over five-day old snow to find the path. Buck was in the very back to make sure no one fell behind. After Vern went, the next one would go, and the next, as we waited our turn to venture from our safety onto the path of danger. For some reason this raddled Dylan and he became befuddled. He was standing in line pounding his boots in the snow.

That didn't bother anybody until he kept it up harder, then harder, mumbling something under his breath, getting louder. The others were moving along this narrow and unforgiving path, as though walking on a tight rope. Trying to get their pace and balance, putting one foot in front of the other like a trapeze artist. The trail wasn't easy. It was hazardous as Hell and took getting used to. Dylan just kept shuffling his feet. Finally, like a cat, Vern came back from the front to talk to him because Dylan was having a tough time watching his dad.

Vern said, "Take it easy, man. We've got a long way to go and you're never going to make it like this. We'll have to leave you and pick you up on the way back."

That seemed to resolve any confusion with young Dylan. His freneticism calmed down and he was forever more the model climber. I was the last in line, but for Buck, and right after Nancy (of course, I couldn't get rid of her).

But come to think of it, she had to be in line, either in front of me or in back, and it is "ladies first" after all.

We divided the survival gear between us, so in addition to carrying my sleeping bag and extra clothes in case of emergency, I carried the communal bowl. This didn't weigh much, but it was big by volume. Starting toward Denali Pass I was feeling competent. That doesn't mean I felt great, but strong and adequate. If given enough time, there was nothing to stop me.

About halfway across the Autobahn the path began to rise more quickly. Every time I took a step, I felt somebody was standing on my air hose. I was puffing and panting, almost hyperventilating. We were at 18,000 feet, with 2,310 feet to go. I couldn't get the rhythm. By the time we reached Denali Pass, I was metaphorically coughing up blood.

I took off my pack and lay to rest on a tiny hill. Fortunately, my recovery time was good. In about five minutes, I looked around to see who was there. There was Nancy, looking at me with bemusement. We had gone off-line, so everyone was free to move on when they felt refreshed, and the others had moved on. Nancy was straightening herself out and ready to roll. Buck had not stopped and moved on. There was nobody there. I was the last one, and that made me feel really bad. Vern turned up again to check what was happening.

"How you feeling?" he said.

"Just catching my breath. I couldn't get in a rhythm, but I'm okay."

"How much of the communal gear you got."

"Just the bowl."

He looked at me long and hard, not smiling. "Well, we got to get going."

"I know. I'm going to make it. It's just a matter of time."

"Your time is taken off. We're starting up the Ridge, that's your time."

He turned and walked away leaving me to struggle with my time. I got the message. There's only so much of it and it's not mine. It's the group's time. I realized for me to stick with the group, I had to step up and hustle. I had to work at it energetically, put my mind to it. I had to push my way with force, be aggressive, put my nose to the grindstone and keep it there. I didn't have the luxury of working at my own pace because I'm too damn slow. I'd get lost in Nancy's snow spray.

I began working in pain far outside my comfort zone; muscles straining, heart pumping, lungs exploding, legs quivering, feet aching, and butt burning. I wanted more of it. I caught up with them in half an hour and was jubilant. Every step I took was to the summit, rushing for the next step. The incident at the pass had spooked me, and I never lagged behind again.

Death on Summit Ridge

The Summit Ridge has a contour that goes up and down like waves as you ascend another 1,000 feet. You're moving up a big rise, and down to a flat floor. Once you've got your stride, the gentle slope down is delightful. It's nothing too dramatic, except you lose oxygen with every step going up. And, well, oxygen is key.

We made it to the Football Field, a large flat expanse of snow, and sat in a circle to restore our energy, talk, and eat lunch. Our lunch had been the same every day: a plastic bag from Talkeetna filled with sandwich, raisins, cookies, and candy. It was getting old! Then, completely out of character with our previous lunches, Vern gets up and walks across the field and out of sight on the other side.

That prompted the group to sit in silence listening to those stinking, nosy crows making a nuisance of themselves. "Why's that?" we asked to the only other person of authority with insight as to where Vern was going: Buck.

Here's the core of what Buck said: "Vern guided a tour to the summit earlier in May, 1988. Fresh from his solo winter ascent in February, he was feeling on top of the world. Had there been a popularity contest in Alaska, Vern would have won. But Vern's a humble person, and to say his new popularity embellished his ego to a degree it affected his decision making would be a mistake."

He'd accomplished something never done before. And it was no small feat. He'd been out there a month and the whole State of Alaska was rooting for him. Listening on their radios, hoping to hear his voice. There was something about the endeavor, to climb Denali solo in Winter, to which every Alaskan can relate. If Verm was thinking he could motivate a person with his *esprit de corps*, to give them the strength to reach the summit to achieve their goal in life, then more power to him.

He made a mistake in judgment though. There was a young woman on his expedition who was a little overweight, not in top condition, but had the heart and soul of a high-altitude climber. She was bursting with enthusiasm, loved everything about the climb. She begged him to let her go to the summit. She made it to the summit camp at 17,500, and she could make it one day more for the summit. She pleaded with Vern to please let her go. She lived her life for this.

Vern, the first man to solo Denali in Winter could handle this. He would watch her closely and at the first sign of fatigue he'd escort her back personally. The guide is responsible for the lives of his clients. The authorities don't allow him to march everyone to their death. But being a guide also comes the critical responsibility of telling a climber they can't go to the summit. Vern was willing to accept that risk in favor of the woman realizing her dream of summitting and going home a star, like Vern.

The girl did great. She kept up, didn't complain, and as far as Vern could tell, she was a regular trooper. The problem was once she struggled to the summit and made her dream come true, she passed out. There was still life in her body, but her mind was gone. Her brain shut off due to oxygen deprivation, no nutrients, the cells had no sugar so her synapses wouldn't snap and her body couldn't function. All that was left was a warm body. And after a couple of hours, that too had passed no matter how many sleeping bags Vern wrapped her in. She froze and was pronounced dead."

Because Vern is similar in authority to a sea captain, or chief, or designated person, he buried her with permission of her parents, near the summit of Denali where he had gone to commemorate. I was up, along with some others, pacing and stomping the snow to keep warm. We roped up to make an orderly approach to the summit and began the trudge across the football field.

To the Summit

Why is the approach to the summit so goddamn long? It's relatively easy, but it's still 20,000 feet high. How long is it? A half mile, a mile? Nobody knows. Keep your head down and breathe. Smooth and steady. Step, take four breaths, step, five breaths, step, six breaths; hell, at the end I was counting 8 breaths, going up that little hill in front of the summit. You must climb 300 more feet before you can enjoy the celebrity of standing on the summit.

STEP. STEP. STEP.

Hooray! We justifiably were on top of the world. We stood at the very top of Mt. McKinley, to be named Denali twenty-eight years later, then renamed Mt. McKinley again. I picked up a small stone the size of my palm and slipped it into my pocket. It was white quartz, round and smooth, I couldn't believe my good fortune. I had my photograph taken with Vern, then Vern and Art, then Vern, Art and Dylan, then with the whole gang. A knoll about three feet high marked the highest part of the mountain. If you were going to be on the absolute peak, you would have to stand on top of that knoll. Christian and Dylan asked me to take their picture, and I was happy to do so. It was fun.

We were so lucky because it was sunny, and the sky was blue when a jet suddenly appeared as a speck in the distance. An F-15 was 150 feet overhead. We got buzzed. Wow! We're having fun now. It was upon us, over us, and gone past, as far into Canada as you could see.

The celebration soon began to wane. It was so cold you wouldn't want to subject your bare skin to the elements. It was probably 10 below zero, not uncommonly cold, but a slap of wind will drop the temp to 40 below. What happens is, the wind will be silent, with a constant breeze blowing lightly, then zap—the tail of the wind will whip up and smack anything you've laid bare into ice.

So it was when, as sort of an afterthought, Nancy asked if I would take a picture of her on the knoll. "Of course," I said after a long hesitation. I stripped my over-mitt off, then my mitten, got down to my gloves and took them off my right hand so I could feel her camera. She climbed up on the knoll and struck a pose. I had the camera up, a little adjustment, and click, she had her photo. Could I take one more? Again, camera up, a little adjustment, and ZAP! The wind caught the very end of my right fingers and burned the hell out of them. That's how I learned it didn't take any time at all to get frostbite. It only takes a second.

When it's time to go, you rope up and go. I was fumbling with the knot on my climbing harness and couldn't get the rope through when Vern grabbed it, fixed it, and barked, "get outta here." For once I was first in line, heading the team home for tea in about four hours. You lose track of time up there. It was late afternoon, the sun was low in the sky, and it seemed there would be plenty of it, but I raced anyway. As we got lower, the sun got lower, and by the time we got to Denali Pass, it was settling on the horizon.

There are not too many times I'm sorry I don't have a camera. I wish I had one there to capture what I saw. A view beyond words gave an ethereal look that put me in another world, one bigger, more striking. I prepared for such moments by traveling around the world without a camera, taking a lasting likeness in my mind. There was no time for a camera here. We were struggling with staying alive in our twelfth or thirteenth hour, and we weren't stopping for pictures.

As we turned the corner at Denali Pass, we were greeted by an open sky from the West Buttress to the Autobahn. The sun was slightly below the horizon, leaving a bright orange stripe around the middle of the earth. Followed by a yellow band, then a diffused white that marked the difference between daytime in one hemisphere to nighttime in another. The white turned to turquoise, and turquoise to black, as it reached the apex of the universe above us. There were millions of stars gathered in the center. This wasn't happening in one spot closest to the sun but shown with equal brilliance across the sky.

The path across the Autobahn was becoming soft because of the sun shining on it all day. It was easy to walk on with crampons and flattened out over the course of the day. I noticed the snow bridge up ahead was not quite right. Maybe it was okay, or maybe it was sagging. I was sure it would be strong enough, until I stepped on it with my boot, and then my leg slowly got swallowed up to my waste, until it broke, and I went dangling 20 feet below in the bowl of the Autobahn. Dylan, who was behind me, thankfully stuck

MT. DENALI

his ice axe in the snow and immediately wrapped the rope around it a couple of times, securing me for the moment, while hanging 2,000 feet above certain death.

"So there you were, hanging 2,000 feet above certain death," to quote Christian, who was second behind Dylan. No truer words had been spoken. They stood there not knowing what to do. There was nobody around to initiate a rescue, so the next best thing was to begin hollering advice.

It was very strange hanging there, face forward on the ice. The ice axe I used to arrest my fall was of no use against the ice wall I faced. It scraped rooster tails but couldn't get a bite. I stopped, then attempted my axe again, this time planting the axe deep in the ice so I wasn't going anywhere. But I couldn't get my feet planted. I was hugging the ice, trying to get a hold with the side of my crampons, but it wasn't working. It was like my legs were pedaling a bicycle, trying to stab the side of the mountain with my crampon each time my boots came around.

I hung onto my axe. It hadn't been a violent fall. When I stepped onto the bridge it broke like melting slush and down I went. Thankfully my fall was restricted to 20 feet. I rested my head on the ice wall and had no idea how to get out of this jam.

Fortunately, Vern did. He materialized out of vapor within seconds. The guy's like superman. He's directly in front of me looking down.

He says, "Turn towards the mountain."

"I'm towards the mountain." I said, because my legs, belly and chest were hugging the mountain. I would've liked to become part of the mountain.

"No, turn your feet towards the mountain and dig in your front crampons."

I did like he said, turned my crampons toward the mountain and kicked in the fangs.

"Now push yourself away from the mountain and climb up."

Let me tell you. When you got nothing but a 95-degree slant of slippery ice underneath you for as far as you can see, that's a tough order to follow. We'd been climbing for fourteen hours, and all I wanted was to not be hanging here. I pushed myself out, stood up on the fangs of my crampons, and stepped up the mountain side as though I was walking to dinner. It was that easy. Easy as pie.

Vern smiled, patted me on the back, and sent me on my way. From then on, I knew how to get out of that jam—one I hoped never to be in again.

Mountains Never Change

There are a lot of things that change over time. They didn't have laptops in 1988. The iPhone changed everything, if there was service. And then there's the whole social media thing. But the physicality of climbing mountains remains the same. There's no easy route. No way to remove the hurt. Mountaineering gear has gotten better, but climbing the mountain still entails putting one foot in front of the other. You can't eliminate the chance of death, or the pain of blisters. Every drop of sweat I perspired is going to be like yours, the result of toil. Nothing changes. These rugged mountains, today, are every bit as rugged as they were in 1988.

Remember the Spaniard we met when we first started our expedition? He was one man, solo. There were no other climbers the whole time we were on the mountain. We were the last ones.

As we descended, we found the Spaniard's tent below Windy Corner, still standing upright, looking normal. There were footsteps in the snow leading away from the tent and up the mountain to the north. The footsteps went one-two, one-two, straight up the side of the hill in a perfect pace. They went straight up and over the hill, disappearing to the other side several hundred feet away. The prints were three, four days old, which meant only one thing, he wasn't coming back.

Vern checked with the ranger station; they were aware of the situation and felt the same way. There was no need for a search and rescue team. There was no need for a retrieval team.

It was his way of committing suicide.

MT. DENALI

Vern & me at the top!

Taking a sunbathing break

Art, me, and Vern

Summit Day

MT. ACONCAGUA, ARGENTINA (1989)

9.

Harmonic Convergence

My friend, Tom Taplin, was asleep in his bag when the snow crushed him. He was lying in his tent at Mt. Everest Base Camp during the Nepal Quake of 2015. On April 25, 2015, the 7.8 earthquake devastated the Himalayan nation of Nepal, causing an avalanche in the mountains above Everest Base Camp.

The percussion of that avalanche exploded into a billowing cloud of tsunami force. One survivor described it as "high as 100 Empire State Buildings." The force blew across the glacier plane leaving a wake of broken dreams in its path. The list of victims included three dead Americans. One of them was Tom Taplin: *climber, filmmaker, and author.*

You must read the *signs* in life to determine how to act next. It's instructive to know that the one person who taught me the most about the will to survive, is killed from an earthquake percussion on the moraine of Mt. Everest's Base Camp, after I saved his life on the moraine of Mt. Aconcagua's Base Camp in 1989, twenty-six years earlier.

Isn't that ironic? I heard about it on the news just as I was beginning to write this memoir. Talk about a sign.

Taplin wrote a book about his escape from death entitled, *Aconcagua: The Stone Sentinel* (1992). In it, he documents his accidental fall into a crevasse and the role I and several other people played in saving him. To preserve the accuracy of the account, he interviewed the three eyewitnesses to his slipping on glacier scree and falling into the crevasse, as well as those at Aconcagua Base Camp who witnessed the rescue operations.

The strength of one's will to survive isn't fathomed until you've seen it working firsthand. Helping someone escape certain death was an honor. When you participate in mountain sports the odds of saving somebody's life become enhanced. Nevertheless, witnessing the fall of a climber, and being the person solely responsible for getting help from three miles away, was task worthy. But navigating the trail entailed maneuvering down ravines and gullies, around gorges, and up and over endless moulins; then leading the rescuers back across the same glacier of giant molehills, to an accident scene you can't see, is at 14,000 feet, and doing it without getting lost, was special.

From Tom Taplin's view, after bouncing like a pinball, slamming side to side against opposite walls of the crevasse, and falling into a foot of icy water sixty feet below, his right arm shattered, he wrote of the experience:

"Once the specter of death became a tangible reality, there was a big debate going on, subconsciously, about just how peaceful death was going to be. As the day progressed and more of the glacier melted, the water level would only get higher and the current stronger. Slowly losing consciousness, then being flushed down the channel was not going to be as peaceful as, say, walking through some beautiful valley, laying down in the snow and going to sleep. So, although the notion of dying was comprehensible, dying beneath a glacier was completely unacceptable.

"From that moment on, all thoughts were directed toward extricating myself from the moulin. My adrenaline and noradrenaline hormones were having a wild party; everything was crystal clear. I was also pissed as hell at myself for being so careless, and that anger had a lot to do with finding a solution. But I had to act fast."

Cat on a Hot Tin Roof

That's where I came in. About ten seconds before Tom slipped beneath the ice, I had yelled to him from 40 yards away, "That looks dangerous. Try the other way," motioning him to the right.

"Okay," he said, as he took two steps to the left. As I told Tom for his book, his left foot slipped from under him and he was gone, very quickly, no chance of saving himself, although he tried. It's strange the things you think at such inopportune times. My reaction was completely detached from his fall. That was due in part because I warned him several times to use caution before his boot slipped on loose gravel.

It was clear he was on dangerous ground; it seemed inevitable something bad was going to happen. Tom was standing on a brown layer of rocks that covered the ice like frosting. He was standing uphill, above the open crevasse without crampons on, for God's sake!

"There he goes," is all I could say. What I saw was a day-hiker in double plastic boots, with his crampons and ice axe in his day pack. When he slipped, his feet stretched out from under him as he hit the scree on his belly and began to claw. Both arms and legs clawed wildly in his futile attempt to keep from going down. But nothing could keep Tom from his fate. A cat sliding off a hot tin roof came to mind. He couldn't get any traction and his arms flailed as he scrambled to save himself.

MT. ACONCAGUA

We stood there; jaws dropped. Borgel and I chose Neil to go for help because he was 21 years old and eager to do the job. His youth made him a reasonable choice because going for help involved making haste over three miles of rough terrain to Base Camp at *Plaza de Mules,* 14,000 ft. We knew our guides would surely have the necessary equipment to save a climber 80 ft. down a crevasse. This was Mt. Aconcagua, the second highest of the Seven Summits at 23,320 ft. We all paid good money for a world class guiding service with a priority on safety.

Five minutes after Neil took off, we realized it made no sense to send only him, especially since we could see him heading in a questionable direction. Taplin's life depended on getting rescued as soon as possible or he would freeze. What would happen if Neil got on the wrong trail and got lost?

You couldn't see Base Camp across the valley and walk to it. You had to find your way along a path that split into many other paths. Out of breath and in a rush, you could get easily turned around. We weren't acclimated yet. We'd been there only one day. What if Neil fell in a crack or down a gorge or sprained an ankle? We hadn't expected this to happen to Taplin. So I decided to go myself, as fast as I could.

I thought at a moment like this, by some miracle of heroism, I would suddenly sprout wings like Pegasus and fly across the glacier for help. That was not to be. There was just me, trying to do my best. I made my strides as long as possible. My speed was measured by the distance to Base Camp divided by my lack of oxygen. Wearing safari shorts, blue long johns, lime green double plastic boots, with purple over-boots up to my knees, I paced each step, head down in full charge.

Altitude made the task equivalent to performing it on top of Mt. Whitney, the highest mountain on the continental United States. If not acclimated, it's like running a marathon with a paper bag over your head. It didn't matter though; I only needed enough breath to give a detailed account of the emergency to the guides and let them handle it. Tom Taplin could be rescued without me.

Upon reaching Base Camp, I was greeted by two surprises.

First, the guides had no ropes. Unfuckingbelievable. No time to argue. It had been determined by our Argentine guide, Enrique, the genius responsible for not bringing a rope to a mountain climbing expedition, that we can use tent sashes to rescue Tom. Wow! They're going to haul Tom up from an 80-foot crevasse with 100-pound sash cords

MT. ACONCAGUA

used to anchor the camp tents. If that's all you got, you sure hope it will hold.

The other problem was they had no harness either! No ropes, no harness. When in doubt, "Do something, even if it's wrong!" People ran to get tent ties and knot them together.

Enrique asked me: "Do you think Taplin's life is in danger?"

Tom had yelled up some barely audible responses before I left. I envisioned him trapped up to his chest in glacier water with a broken arm, ice walls straight up both sides blocking the sun, with no way out. So yes, time is of the essence. "Yes, he's in danger (you fucking idiot). Go get him!"

Then I got my second surprise. No way could I explain to Enrique which crevasse Tom was trapped in. There must be a million 'moulin' across the moraine that all look alike. From Base Camp, you look out over an entire ocean of rolling brown knolls with shady dips. The ice is covered with a gravel crust so thick you don't realize there is a glacier underneath. Sub-glacier streams cut ravines under the ice which merge into gorges and channels. As the glacier moves down the valley, the ice cracks, and sheared walls reveal the seductive blue ice luring climbers to it.

I am the only person who knows where Tom is. Across that treacherous sea of undulating teats, a man's life is teetering on my ability to lead the rescuers to him. All eyes were on me.

"You must lead us back," said Enrique.

What a horrible development! Physically and mentally, I'd hit my wall and was spent. I did my duty to deliver the message, "Tom needs help!" the same way as Pheidippides ran from Marathon to Athens, then fell dead after delivering his fateful message. I was exhausted. Where the hell was Neil?

Neil had gotten lost. In Neil's own words from Tom's book, *Aconcagua: The Stone Sentinel,* he stated:

"That was a shitty time for me. Even though I had still not recovered from the day before, I was running as fast as I could, with double plastic boots which is not an easy thing to do. I took several face plants. I thought, I don't care what happens...I might get really sick, but I have to hurry.

I knew for a fact that Taplin was having a rough time. There was this image of him in my mind – a 'freeze memory' – before he dropped over the edge and free-fell into the crevasse; I could see him going down and I could see the color of his ice-axe.

I saw the trail leading up to Camp 1 from Base Camp and decided to head for that reference point, thinking it would be quicker to take a straight route across the moraine instead of following the path—which did not turn out to be true at all. At one point I had to descend a gully and cross a stream which blocked my view of the Camp 1 trail — 'Way to go, Neil. It's not my fault Taplin's had an accident. Now I've really blown everything.'"

I last saw Neil far, far away from the path I was taking around the basin to camp. He looked about an inch tall on the horizon. He was stumbling like a soldier across the terrain, hell bent in the resolve of his final charge. His arm rose in recognition, before he fell forward, flat to the ground.

The Rescue

Beyond rising to the occasion, the problem with taking the rescue team back was I had to think; and there was no blood in my brain for that. I was thinking about how I wanted to save Tom's life. But the motivation to save another man's life is not as strong as the will to save your own. I was not embraced by the same will to live as Tom, and I fully recognized the irony in that statement. But I was worn ragged. The thought of trekking back three miles in altitude, in a big hurry, as though someone's life depended on me, made me want to throw up.

Be that as it may, I pressed on. But which way? We could not go back the way I came along the basin. Every second counted now, so we had to go straight over the Moulin. I would look for any familiar landmark, estimate distance and direction, then calculate a dead reckoning to Tom, or thereabouts. The guides waited anxiously. Once I navigated a course, the guides took off ahead of me to look for a *sign*, any kind of sign, but there was none. We did that over and over again.

Enrique expected me to fly like an arrow to the accident site. But these operations went on for at least half an hour —calculating and recalculating on the run, searching for a pinnacle or ice patch, or any identifying feature in the middle of this sea of moving parts. We came to a confusing juncture on the moraine, where several paths met in a hub that split like spokes on a giant Catherine's wheel.

It was crucial to the rescue that I knew which path to take, but I couldn't figure it out. Fear and frustration loomed large in my stomach, and in my mind, but nothing came. Enrique stood there gaping at me in anticipation. Pepe took off like a crazed ape up the Moulin, and I appreciated his efforts. It meant somebody beside me was doing something to find Tom.

I was huffing and puffing, trying to focus and collect my thoughts. I needed blood for my brain. I needed some luck. Then I got it. A smile came to my face when I recognized the right fork on the pinwheel, the connection was made tying all loose ends together, identifying the final leg of the rescue. I shouted to Pepe. He and Enrique ran like the world-class climbers they were supposed to be, in the direction I pointed. That path converged at the sight of Borgel standing on a ridge a couple of hundred yards away. I was amazed that he could not be seen earlier. I dropped to the ground and panted.

By then, Tom had almost saved himself but *almost* wasn't good enough. If rescuers had not arrived, Borgel could have done nothing but watch him die. With his one arm disabled by his fractures, Taplin put his crampons on single-handedly, grabbed his ice axe and did something he had never done before. Like the madman he had become, he went berserk and attacked the blue ice with everything he had—and "front-pointed."

Pulling on his ice axe with both arms, he front-pointed straight up the glacier wall forty feet to a foot wide ledge. From there he was still thirty feet below the rim where Borgel was watching his every move. And that's where Tom stood for forty-five minutes, shaking viciously from hypothermia, waiting for somebody to save him. He was shaking so violently he looked like he might fall back into the crevasse at any moment.

Here's Taplin, *"When I first got to the ledge I knew I'd cheated death and had won that round. I looked down into the Moulin and tried to figure out how many lives I had left. But it was stupid to think I was home-free; I was only half way out and the beast was still there, waiting with open jaws. I was still trapped. All my effort seemed pointless; all that focus and adrenaline which had allowed me to get to the ledge deemed to dissolve into a kind of wasted, hypothermic numbness."*

Here's Borgel: *"Even after Taplin made it to the ledge I was real scared because I knew I could still not get to him. I felt so helpless because I could not do a damn thing to help him get out. I've never been in a situation like that. It was the first time I've felt somebody was going to die when I was the only person right there."*

~

Tom Taplin did cheat death that day in 1989, and given his mountainous lifestyle, he probably cheated it a few times before his life was up 26 years later. When Tom was hit with that percussion blow at Mt. Everest Base Camp, he was sleeping in his tent and didn't feel anything. He experienced what we call a *good* death—to die in a natural disaster on Mt. Everest is any climber's dream death. Providing they are old enough.

I promise you this about myself:

I'm the guy who will not fall into the crevasse. I can sense danger and will warn you away. If your life depends on my going for help, I'm the guy who will not get lost on the moraine. I will get you help and do whatever is necessary to complete the task. I will find my way back over any circumstances, using dead reckoning if necessary. I am your friend. I will not give up and you will live.

MT. ACONCAGUA, ARGENTINA (1989)
10.
Highest Peak in Northern/Southern Hemisphere

Aconcagua is nothing like Denali. In fact, it's the complete opposite. On Denali you're always on 6,000,000 acres of ice and snow, on Aconcagua you're always on dirt or rocks. It's always white on Denali, on Aconcagua it's always brown. On Denali you're always clean, and on Aconcagua you're covered in dust and dirt. That makes a world of difference when it comes to your feet.

If you let a little blister grow into a big blister, one upon the other, blister upon blister, you'll be in Hell. Blisters have their own unique pain, or call it torture. It's not life threatening (hell, it's four feet from your heart) but feels like a burning hole, not in your feet, but in your brain. When you're growing blisters across the balls of your feet to your little toe, then back down your heels, on both sides, you don't have to be reminded what an idiot you are. On Aconcagua, I was that idiot.

We were ferrying gear from base camp at *Plaza de Mulas* (14,337 feet), skipping Camp Canada at (16,108 ft.), depositing our loads at *Nido de Condores* (17,500 feet) and

MT. ACONCAGUA

coming back to base camp to sleep at night—all in the effort to acclimatize. This is a very boring leg of the climb, made twice as bad by having to continue pass the 'normal' Camp Canada, and heading up the switchbacks some 3,313 feet. It's walk, walk, turn left; then walk, walk, turn right, and on you go until you reach *Nido*. That's a lot of elevation to hump your load when not acclimatized, or even if you are.

The blisters developed coming down the mountain. Blisters are not to be ignored. You should stop and immediately remedy the pain. I thought I was okay because I wore the same plastic boots six months earlier climbing up and down Denali and never had a problem with my feet. I discovered it was because I was walking on snow and ice the entire time. Each time I stepped, the boot would push down into the snow, which absorbed the friction that occurred from the plastic boot rubbing on my heels.

On Aconcagua, without the cushion of snow to absorb the *downward* thrust of my boot, it would stop immediately on rock, causing my heel to slide up and down inside the boot. For 3,313 vertical feet my heel rubbed on the back of the boot making a fire of friction. The balls of my feet jammed into the back of my toes, causing blood to pool.

The outcome was disastrous because I didn't stop even once to look. The half-dollar size blisters erupted from the top-skin of my heel rubbing on the under-skin at the heel: getting bigger as the cells burst into flames. And the dollar-size blood blisters on the balls of my feet kept making more blisters as I walked, piling on top of each other. Triple blisters. Never saw anything like it. I had on thick wool socks, a polypropylene pair, and a thin pair which perhaps spared me from getting something worse, but I don't know what that could be.

A sterile needle was needed to puncture the top skin of the blood blisters so they could drain on both feet, then I started to cut off the skin -- thinking better of it when I saw the pink tissue underneath. I left it alone. In the end, the experience cost me a world of hurt. I was fortunate the next day was a rest day to give my feet the break. I cut-up some mole skin to place over the blisters but that didn't work, it rubbed right off. All I could do was wait and see how it works on tomorrow's climb.

The next day turned out to be a day of rancor, just like the blisters. The expedition showed signs of discontent and bitterness. The first issue was the size of the group. There were eighteen of us and three guides. Frustrating as that issue was, two of the guides didn't speak English. So,

MT. ACONCAGUA

with no ability to communicate, they sat in their tent all day and drank wine until it was time to eat—and it wasn't a big tent. And it seconded as our mess hall.

Some of us would crowd in the tent to get served and some of us wouldn't, which led to the second problem, no food. And the third problem: Why are we skipping Camp Canada when the itinerary clearly stated that was a designated stop?

Let me unravel this fiasco for you, so when you hear how Dr. Anil Patel fell off the mountain on his traverse to the *Canaleta* —falling 1,000 feet, breaking his ribs, his hip, dislocating his right arm, and suffering brain damage from smacking his head on rocks so severely he lost his license to practice medicine—you'll understand how it could have been avoided.

When you look up expeditions to Mt. Aconcagua you find most injuries are limited to altitude sickness and cold weather problems. Should I feel lucky I survived an expedition that experienced two near death fatalities? A roster of the players would be helpful.

The first group is made up of the Family Gould, or "Swiss Family Robinson," as we called them. Mr. Gould was the 65-year-old patriarch of the family. A former Yale attorney, he suffered from not having control over the situation. Mary "Mumsy" Gould was the 65-year-old matriarch. I spoke to her once as we trekked to *Mulas*, the base camp, and found she was heavily protected from the outside influences, such as myself, by her two scions: Her son, Kingdom "King" Gould, III, the 40-year-old "ne'er do well," who was married and had two children, and last was the daughter, Annunziata "Nunzy" Gould, the fair-haired princess of them all at 29 years old.

They were a unit unto themselves, prepared to go independently with their own food supply and cooking gear, if necessary. Mr. Gould and King made their first attempt on Aconcagua in 1986, when they reached a highpoint of 19,000 feet. They were all very much aloof, but still part of the team under the leadership of Enrique.

The second group was made up of street mountaineers who were all business. They took this climb seriously and acted like it. They were Craig Roland, a 55-year-old architect from Santa Rosa, CA. He was tall and slender, ran marathons, and was indefatigable in his backpacking through the Sierra, clearly the strongest member of us all. He came with his friend, Bill English, 44 years old, a quiet man and owner of an art supply store. Dick Gordon, 32 years old, single, there was some question about his status as a paying customer. He helped the guides while maintaining his aloneness. Seemed competent and confident, he had a way of acting very military like, so we called him "Corporal." He was the one member that remained loyal to the expedition's management—Enrique.

There was Thomas Borgel, a 30-year-old manufacturing engineer, and his best friend Greg Lewis, a 32-year-old aeronautical engineer, two Georgia crackers that laughed and joked a lot. The meaning of the climb was not lost on them, but they weren't wasting time thinking about it. Neil Delahey, 21 years old, and his best friend Trevor Byles, 22 years old, both just graduated from the University of Colorado. Young, naive, and full of energy, they were both ready and eager to go to the summit.

Tom Taplin, who fell in the crevasse, was special in his own way. He was comfortable with anybody. I learned from him how much more a photo/journalist must do to get the right shots. When you see the picture of the first man shaking hands with the second on top of the mountain, it's because a guy like Tom had already pulled ahead and climbed to the top to photograph it.

Then there was the odd group. Mike Milford was a 55-year-old Pole, proud of his heritage and friendly—but angry and confused over the situation he seemed not to understand. He was from New York, along with his friend

Greg Staciak, 26 years old. They arrived late from the plane and barely caught the group bus to *Puente del Inca*. Mike was not in the shape he wanted to be. He was garrulous by nature but never quite got up to speed. Greg Staciak should never have been on this climb. He still had on a dress shirt and penny loafers at *Puente del Inca*.

The third member of this odd group was Dr. Anil Patel, a 41-year-old anesthesiologist based at South Hampton Hospital on Long Island, married with two daughters. This man was truly odd. I had long talks with him at the beginning of this expedition in Mendoza and everything he said was wrong, particularly when it came to his equipment. His boots, for example, came from a climb he was on in 1967, twenty-two years earlier. They wouldn't have been the right boots if they were new, but to expect to climb the highest mountain in the Northern and Southern Hemisphere in those boots was crazy. He may as well have worn old toasters on his feet. That's how dried up, crinkly, and tattered those boots were. I urged him to go buy new expedition boots that first day. Anil had no comprehension of what "horrendous conditions" meant. He promised he would be fine, but he ended up borrowing a pair of "Bunny Boots" from Enrique, and his old boots ended up in my pack when we got back to the hotel after the climb. Go figure.

Nobody attempted to identify themselves in the group as we started to gather for the climb at the hotel. It was eighteen different people looking at each other, wondering if they could all just get along. The knot was that eighteen people were bigger than a group—it was approaching a mob. At the first 'meet up' at the Grand Balbi Hotel in Mendoza, steps should have been taken to introduce each member of the group, making it fun, like a friendly camp counselor would do. Take the starch out of the linen.

But Enrique was not like that. His presentation was terse, his English met only the basic requirements and his concern for a personal check of the gear was none. His disgust for Neil and Trevor showing up drunk at the meeting was apparent, and after briefly outlining our schedule for the next few days, it was over. Eighteen people left to feel uncomfortable, while sizing each other up.

Delusion of Grandeur

From Mendoza, the next stop was *Puente del Inca*, a three-hour bus ride taking us to the main lodge before starting the hike at 9,000 feet. The Goulds hired a minibus for themselves the day before, further severing any hope for a group bond. But the whole group came together for one big photo of solidarity. It was the last time we were all together, everybody except the Goulds.

One of the most important experiences on these climbs is comradery. On the human side, that's what it's all about—people working together for a common goal. Enrique mentioned splitting up the group. I couldn't wait to divide up so we could start talking more personally, getting to know people. A large group does not enhance friendship. It takes intimacy out of any relationship; that's the nature of the herd mentality. Nine people can be interesting, while eighteen people are boring.

It never gets better than the beginning when you are swelling with excitement. I was laughing my ass off at the group dinner in the Lodge, on the verge of being silly I was so excited in anticipation. Happy to be part of the whole group of 'wannabe' climbers willing to put their life on the line to summit Mt. Aconcagua. Me, and whoever I was talking to, were looking forward to what's going to happen next. The whole adventure was in front of us. We were having one of the times of our lives.

We started off the next day with the mules carrying our packs, and us in shorts with light day packs. As we set out across the plains to the mountains, we were spared the abuse of high desert wind. It was warm and pleasant. From the Lodge at *Puente del Inca* to base camp at *Plaza de Mulas,* is twenty-six miles, with a 5,000-foot gain. We were climbing about 192 feet per mile. That's not a challenging climb, in fact, it's not a climb at all, but it is 26 miles. The trail runs through the Horcone Valley, making the day eventful if there are problems crossing the two rivers. For us it was uneventful. We were lucky.

We made camp at *Confluencia*, the junction where the water run-off meets between the Superior and Inferior Horcone glaciers far up the valley. Our campsite was atop a plateau with a crystal-clear stream running through camp that you could jump across. Little tufts of grass grew along the edge of the stream; you could get in your sleeping bag and snuggle in the long-haired grass. This is the last vegetation you'll see on the climb until you pass this way again. When morning comes it will bring a wide expanse of nothing but desert.

The Horcone Valley is as barren as Afghanistan. The mountains shaping the valley are like those on the moon, with age old deformities. Mammoth boulders lie on the plain, sandstone slabs are turned upside down, and erosion gullies with rockslides are everywhere. It's a barren wilderness that spans all around you.

But that night at *Confluencia*, I nestled my head in a tuft of green grass and watched the stars fill the sky, an errant meteor careening off one to another. I dreamed of standing on the summit of Aconcagua, ice axe in hand, my arms in a triumphant thrust: I was at the top.

MT. ACONCAGUA, ARGENTINA (1989)

11.

The Shit Storm

I told of the incident involving Tom Taplin after we reached *Plaza de Mulas* and ventured out to the *Pinnacles*. A new Hotel was built in the vicinity of that camp site which alleviated some of the stress over the crowded conditions and resulting filth of the place. But let's be clear on how it was before the use of a modern convenience like a hotel. (I'll believe it when I see it.)

Just south of the campground the terrain begins to roll downhill to the glacier run-off. There was an area everyone went to shit. In the height of tourism there could be as many as 700 butts looking to defecate. Fortunately for us, there were only about 100 climbers present in February of 1989.

It was a putrid reality, and I bring it up because I was victimized by the putridity. There was no clean spot to go unless you were willing to take a hike and go out of camp. But sometimes you get caught by surprise with certain time limitations. So, you go to the side of a big hill covered in shit. I daintily walk out onto this minefield of shit. You step here, and then over there, and "Oh, yes, I see a spot, just beyond that toilet paper."

You hop over to a two-foot square to take your shit. You work off the layers of clothing you're wearing and do your business. But wiping can be tricky, you're on a hill and it takes a certain sense of balance, you've got only a couple of feet to manipulate your body and... whoosh! I lost my balance, then, SPLAT!... I was wearing my new camp slippers, big and bulky and full of down, and now they were covered in shit smeared across the bottom. Borgel happened to have his camera and the picture he took said it all. Guys love to tell their biggest shit stories while standing around camp waiting for dinner, and Borgel, Trevor, Neil, Greg and I got a big yuk out of that one—the rest of the camp, not so much.

After the "fubar" evacuation of Taplin, ending with him having to rough ride to Mendoza on a horse that appeared from nowhere, the camp settled down from the excitement of the rescue. It was time to address the subject at hand: we were preparing to ferry the communal gear and food up to *Nido de Condores* the next day—the siege technique, with a sour Alpine twist.

How did it help us to acclimatize by passing Camp Canada at 16,000, and heading for *Nido* at 17,500? The

MT. ACONCAGUA

altitude at 16,000 was perfect. It was marked on the company's brochure as the recommended elevation to spend the night. The 2,000-foot gain from *Mulas* to Canada was plenty for a day's acclimatization. When questioned about it, Enrique was adamant, "I know this mountain. It's best to go up fast."

Vern Tejas wouldn't have agreed, but he wasn't running this show. None of us had climbed from 14,000 straight to 17,500, so how did we know the price we were paying. When I climbed Mt. Cook later, we climbed 5,500 ft. vertical gain, but that was at 12,000 ft. level. We couldn't appreciate the difference between the 16,000-foot camp and the one at 17,500, nor the lasting effects it would have on our bodies.

Enrique knew the difference, and for many of us it proved malignant. What started out as an enthusiastic team of climbers in the morning, turned into a fatigued group of splintered mountaineers in the evening. Divide and conquer. We became a mix of lone climbers racked with altitude deprivation, strewn across the mountain every which way, lost in the dark with varying degrees of pulmonary edema.

The trail is four feet wide, all you do is walk up. But when I hit Camp Canada and realized there was 1,500 more feet to go, serious doubts arose in my brain. It was as though Enrique had grabbed me by the throat and was squeezing my uvula. His grip tightening as he yelled, "I know this mountain. I've been up and down it dozens of times. This is how you climb it!"

Greg Staciak could not have disagreed more. Roland, Dick, Trevor and Neil had no problem making the grade to *Nido*. The 'Swiss Family Robinson' made it in due course, but Enrique insisted Nunzie and Mumsy not carry any load. Borgel, Lewis, and I made it by sucking wind.

As you reach the top of the plateau at 17,000, you hike the last 500 vertical feet through an ice field. It should be called 'Heartbreak Field.' I'm not proud of the way I fell into *Nido* camp and dropped my gear. It was sloppy, but I got there. Then I created the blister problem on my way down by turning up the speed and scorching my feet.

Life threatening problems hampered Milford and Staciak. By the time Staciak got to the ice field his motor skills had deteriorated substantially. It was 7:00 at night and daylight was deteriorating with him. He would take a few steps, then sit down. His face was pale, his breathing shallow and fast, his legs were shaking from fatigue.

Dick and a guide named Gustavo, who couldn't speak English, finally came to Staciak's rescue. They tied a rope around his waist and led him down indignantly to base camp—very slowly, as though he was a crippled child. The rest of the group had been down for hours, coping with different phases of whatever mountain sickness afflicted them. I was dealing with blisters, Borgel a headache, Lewis couldn't eat, Bill Parish stumbled straight into his tent to vomit and shit his pants, and Mike Milford missed a turn in the dark and nearly fell off the edge of the mountain. He got back to camp around midnight, worried sick over his friend and wondered with the rest of us if Staciak hadn't found a place to lie down and die.

No Camp Canada

"Everyone looks tired today, so we'll have another rest day at base camp," Enrique announced. He had no choice; he was risking a mutiny. Craig, Bill, Borgel, Lewis, and I wanted to know again why we passed on Camp Canada. Having lugged our loads and experienced the pain, we wanted to know what we were getting in return. The benefit of using the siege technique on Aconcagua included a night at Camp Canada, it was in the itinerary and Enrique had eliminated this important acclimation stage of our climb. We were livid.

Our bodies, including the muscles, the heart, the absorption system, needed a night to grow and adapt, and not get taxed again by going 17,500 feet into the death zone. If we had to, we could split into two teams, each team according to fitness, make the adjustments and move on. That's how this trip was advertised in the shiny brochure. Three guides to every eight climbers, fifteen days. There were seventeen of us with three guides. The group was unwieldy. We were on our seventh day, so what's the rush? We had eight days left

"No Camp Canada! There will be no Camp Canada! I know this mountain better than anybody, this is the best way to climb it. No, no, no. We go to *Nido*. That will be much better."

Much better for who? Enrique had his reasons, not least of which was we needed food and somebody to cook it for seventeen people. But with his rebuttal sounding so defiant, we looked at each other and shook our heads, "What'd he say?" This was the beginning of a major breakdown in communication, and nobody was listening.

As we saw it, Enrique had no sense of humor. He also had no patience, and no mental ability to fluctuate with the ebb and flow and surges that comes with mountain climbing. He consistently took a statement said in English and misinterpreted it with a connotation in Spanish which led to hard feelings, and decisions based on poor communication.

Both treks to *Nido* were horrific. I don't say that much, but it was the toughest hiking I've ever done. The oxygen deprivation was taxing, but at 17,500 you get only half the oxygen you get down in Mendoza. Maybe it was a psychological thing because I knew Camp Canada at 16,000 just felt right. Above that elevation, there was a demonstrative slow down with my body; it hit a wall, and I didn't want to press on.

This took me aback because I expected to be fresher on this climb due to my workout schedule. For the last two months I'd been running fifty stadium climbs a day in my double plastic boots, five miles of cardio four days a week, and weights three times a week. I was in shape, but not acclimating the way I should, the way I had on Denali.

The acclimation process can be different every time. On Denali we used the siege technique, and it took us eighteen days before we reached 17,500 feet. On Aconcagua, we had been on the mountain for seven days to reach that same elevation: eleven days less. It occurred to me Enrique didn't know how to execute the proper siege technique, being he was Argentinian. He knew nothing about the American way of laying siege, bringing in sufficient supplies of food and having the patience to outlast the mountain's guile before you attack the summit.

Enrique was thinking, we'll go to *Nido,* rest for the day, then push hard the last two days for the summit. Enrique made it happen that way by shortening the rations. Enrique only brought enough food to feed eight climbers out of the seventeen climbers remaining on the trip. Unbeknownst to us, there was no plan to feed nine of us for the remaining eight days of the trip, thereby guaranteeing that the climb wouldn't last more than three days.

I was one of the last to come stumbling into *Nido de Condores* after that grueling second carry. It gave me time to think about leadership. The leader, whoever he or she may be, leads you up the mountain by assisting you on the trail, by supplying gear or giving you a hand. They support you with incantations or advice or forcing you to take the right path if need be. They do not sequester themselves inside their tent, then come out in the morning and point their finger to the summit.

Once I got to *Nido,* I sat down leaning against a rock to relax. I was pleasantly surprised when my body responded rapidly; I could breathe normally in about ten minutes. But I seriously questioned my ability to make the summit. If I was going to the top, it would be the hardest thing I've ever done. I needed a leader. But there wasn't one. So, I came to the stunning conclusion that I'd have to do it myself.

Try Again as You Might

It was Anil Patel and Mike Milford who started the morning of the second carry by leaving base camp at 7:00 without breakfast, arriving at *Nido* around 3:00 in the afternoon. Staciak made the wise decision not to go further. His adventure was over. Anil took Mike under his wing and encouraged the older and slower man he could make the summit. Mike was aware that accelerating his own pace was an invitation to high altitude sickness and didn't want to be rushed. He reported to us he had no headache and was completely acclimatized.

Staciak kept their tent, so Mike was waiting around on the plateau to be assigned to another tent. The plateau is about three football fields large. It is the usual garbage pit, not as bad as *Mulas.* There were pools of water reflecting on the barren rock, and scattered snow patches about the landscape. The plateau is set against the mountain, which points toward the summit in the distance. The trail leading up to the summit is made of arid, windswept, inhospitable mountainsides.

Mike got chilled from not moving around, pulled out his sleeping bag and got in wearing everything, including his parka. The weather was constantly changing, this time for the worst. Swirls of wind with flurries catching the snow and dragging it around; waiting in your bag was not a bad idea.

When Enrique got to camp, he perceived Mike's action as a sign of exhaustion, and told Mike, "I suggest you go down. If you continue to go higher, you may have to walk alone, and I will have to assist you. I cannot spare anybody in case somebody else needs assistance."

What Mike heard, after hiking his heart out all day was, "Mike, you ignorant piece of shit, you look like death and must go down. You've become a burden to everybody, I cannot spare myself to assist you. The other climbers are more important. It's not fair."

What Mike wanted to hear was, "Good job, I'm sure you can sleep with Neil and Trevor tonight."

Mike was fighting mad when he got around to talking with me. He wanted to knock Enrique's teeth out, kick his ass, smother him under a pillow. I laughed because he was shouting loud enough for everyone to hear, and who could get that mad unless they were ready to climb?

I suggested he talk to Enrique again, reasonably, and see what tomorrow will bring. But he wanted no part of appeasement. Enrique belted him a low blow and it sucked the life out of him. He was totally disappointed, his confidence was shaken, and his mental faculties couldn't handle the strain of the emotional roller coaster. It was so long Mike Milford. Enrique thought nothing of it.

When speaking of Mt. Aconcagua, you can always use the words "beautiful" and "dramatic" but you'd be hard pressed to find a place more desolate and exposed than *Nido de Condores*. The quality of food served by the guides went the same way as the landscape. You could never tell what the broth coming from the bowels of the guides' tent would taste like. Maybe it was a "bowl of freeze-dried pasta noodles in clam sauce." Lewis said it was his favorite meal.

Even if you found the meal tasty, there was nowhere to eat it. You're on a windswept mountainside with nothing to hide behind for protection from the wind. We returned to our tents, which were located on the far side of the camp, away from the others. We didn't like listening to them talk and they didn't want to hear us play "crazy eights" or "spades." We always got loud.

I was tent mates with Lewis and Borgel. Neil and Trevor were frequent visitors in what became the last bastion of hope and fortitude. We kept each other going, laughing as much as possible, and encouraging if the mood got serious. Then we went a step further and after the climb we took a vacation to the white sand beaches of Valparaiso, Chile. It's touted as an international destination, but like so many of South America's treasures this paradise had a large sign warning visitors: ocean water polluted.

I lost 25 pounds on this climb. That's a serious weight loss and an indication of the nutritional benefit of our meals, if we had one. It was different from my other expeditions. I am not a picky eater, but *I had no food the last three days* of the climb, along with Lewis and Borgel, and others.

The most memorable day of getting starved came the very last day of the climb, the day we walked out from *Plaza de Mulas* to *Puente del Inca*, a 26-mile stretch. When we woke up that morning, Enrique and Pepe had left for Mendoza with Anil, no one was around except Gustavo. He was sitting in a tent next to a big pot of hot water, with nothing to put in it.

We hiked twenty-six miles on a bowl of hot water. We spent half a day grumbling about how an army marches

MT. ACONCAGUA

on its stomach; the other half of the day we spent laughing about it.

Meanwhile, there were more rumblings of discontent over at the tent of 'Swiss Family Robinson.' The family was about to squabble. Mr. Gould had the mistaken belief he was leading his own expedition. When the altitude got too thin, so did his children's tempers as they began to lose focus on the family unit.

Enrique pitched the guide's tent on the only rock outcropping on the plateau. He advised Mr. Gould to pitch his tent near Enrique's for better food service. Mr. Gould didn't need that advice because he was the trailblazer of his own expedition, thank you, and he wanted his camp someplace else. He would find a place with a level spot for Mumsy's sleeping and advise Enrique.

The plateau is formed in the shape of one plateau layered on top of another and is not made for level sleeping. At a stage in Mr. Gould's attempt to compound the futility of trying to make the rock surface level, it got dark. A storm started to blow in, and the wind began to howl, a nightmare for putting up tents. The Gould's were tired, and Nunzie wanted to lie down and sleep—not an unreasonable request. Her request came out like, "Hey guys we're not at home. We're camping. Just pitch the tent. Let's not try to excavate Aconcagua." Then King started hollering at his dad, "If you want me to help you, do it this way."

Unfortunately for the children, altitude had gotten to Dad too. He announced this was his plight and he would do it his way. Nunzie got frustrated and stomped away for some much-needed quiet time, and King shut up and did like his dad told him. Chalk one up for the old man.

But the one that needed a firm talk was Dr. Anil Patel. Everybody on the climb, except Craig, Neil, Trevor and Dick, had some kind of injury or malady that was torturing them. We weren't camping, we were surviving. Diarrhea and headaches were most common, nausea and digestive problems hampered Mr. Gould, Bill, and Borgel, and Enrique would have had a shit fit if not for Mr. Gould's "Lomotil."

But for us climbers who huffed and puffed to get community water from frozen ponds, it was like going on a weekend trip with Ganga Din. Under Enrique's directions, the clean water came from ponds a couple of hundred meters away, that stayed frozen until late afternoon. Finding the clean water in those frozen ponds became a fiasco, again. "Clean water, yes, right over there, two hundred yards," so says Enrique.

MT. ACONCAGUA

We trekked as far as we could in good conscience. Afterall, we had to carry the water back in open buckets, sloshing all the way. It made for a wet trip home, with ice forming on your trousers like somebody threw water on you. And it was cold at 17,500 feet, even at mid-day it registered 25 degrees. People had their Gore-Tex jackets with their hoods secured tightly around their faces to keep out the wind.

But not Dr. Patel. As he stood contemplating the summit, he had on his ever-present black and white flannel shirt, untucked and unbuttoned to the belly, with red thermal long-johns underneath. He stood gazing out as though nothing was going on around him, no hat or anything on his head, just him staring.

This caught my eye, and I began watching him. Later he was sitting cross legged, covered in yellow plastic rain gear, by himself. I can't fault the guy for purchasing his rain gear at the gas station while on the way to the airport heading for Mendoza, but his choice of equipment indicated he was either stupid or real poor. Since I knew he was neither, it meant he wasn't playing with a full deck or was one brick light of a full load.

Based on my previous experience with Anil in Mendoza, I knew he was a strange bird. But he was the MD, and that was enough authority for him not to listen to anybody who wasn't. He said he grew up at 6,000 feet, and climbed Mt. Kenya 17 times, and Kilimanjaro three times, and had never been bothered by elevation. But now, here he was acting odd, and Enrique was allowing him to continue, probably because he was the doctor.

It turned out most of the 'would-be' mountaineers were taking Diamox to help them acclimatize. I have nothing against drugs, but I felt that being on the mountain was no time to begin experimenting with my blood system. It's also a bit ironic, if not hypocritical, if you believe the point of climbing mountains is to test your body's limits against the hardships Nature can offer.

I asked Dr. Patel to explain how Diamox helps him: "The higher you go up the mountain, reduced atmospheric pressure and lack of oxygen causes changes in the blood gases. Diamox inhibits the enzyme carbonate anhydrate and increases the acidity in the blood by favorably excreting bicarbonate. Diamox, being a diuretic as well as an alkalizing agent, helps to counter some of the effects of carbon dioxide loss caused by rapid breathing at high altitude. It increases blood oxygen levels and helps you keep breathing regular."

I told him, anybody that takes Diamox is a fag.

MT. ACONCAGUA, ARGENTINA (1989)

12.
Night Turns into Day

That night we were blessed with a gorgeous sunset. Earlier in the afternoon there was an incredible thunderstorm. A big storm with huge bolts of lightning breaking through the cumulus clouds, then shooting straight down to the ground, causing horizontal red light to reflect off the snow on the mountain tops, called the "alpenglow" and it's a spectacular phenomenon.

The more you climb big mountains, the more you hear "the mountain creates its own weather." This is due to the incredible size of the mountain, how its mere presence affects the high and low pressure of the currents whirling around it. It's also why you can't predict the weather. "It turns on a dime." A sunny day turns into a blizzard within minutes. It shoots out of the blue sky and "gives you ten cents change."

The next morning, we closed camp at Nido and treaded on to White Rock, our summit camp. The trail up from *Nido* turns around to the northwest edge of the *Gran Acarreo* and follows the ridge to camps Berlin and White

Rock. The *Gran Acarreo* is that massive bulk of upper mountain which sweeps down into a semi-basin of loose stones—a humongous slope of scree. You don't want to go there. You want to stay up toward Berlin at 19,500, or keep moving to White Rock, 700 vertical feet further.

700 vertical feet doesn't sound much further, but after you trek 2,000 vertical feet to Berlin and now have five percent less air, it's a motherfucker. But the problem with Camp Berlin was that it grossly stank of urine. I couldn't smell the urine if you put a cup of it under my nose at the time; I'm not sure why. But Nunzie could smell it, as she so richly pointed out and announced, "We'll all die of urine-halation!" (Ha, ha, ha)

I was for stopping right there but didn't express my opinion because I didn't have the breath to waste. What's another 700 feet? That's an hour less walking in the morning. We pressed on.

Before we left *Nido* that morning, I personally saw Enrique try to stop Anil. It wasn't a talk or debate or conversing about Anil going to White Rock, it was Enrique telling him he must go down. Or was he? Anil was putting on the Bunny Boots Enrique loaned him. Bunny Boots are made completely of consolidated rubber, from the top of their calf-high length to the tips of the toes. They were used for the military, then reproduced in white and made popular when introduced on the Alaskan pipeline to keep the workers' feet from freezing.

They were a solid set of footwear if your motive was to keep your feet from getting frostbite. But they were not a mountain climbing boot and certainly not suitable for climbing Aconcagua. Walking in them was clumsy. They were like space boots in high heels, and you had to walk like well, a …bunny. But worse than that was how they made your feet sweat. All the moisture stayed in the rubber boot and made your feet wrinkly.

Why Enrique loaned him those boots remains a mystery.

Day Turns into Night

Whatever the case, Anil managed to drag himself into White Rock at 19,700 feet. The bad news was we still had 3,000 feet to go. Going high on Aconcagua is like going to the ends of the earth, working through the rubble, with a long line of carcasses along the trail. There was even a dead horse below Camp Berlin at 19,000 feet. I didn't know a horse could go that high, I guess they're not supposed to.

People aren't meant to go that high either. This expedition was nothing like the five clients and two guides struggling against nature for 21 days on Denali. There, we worked as one. Here, there were fifteen clients and three guides to herd them as far up Aconcagua as possible. They may as well have been herding cats.

Tempers were short as we struggled in the altitude, trying our best to set up our tents. Every time you bent over and stood up, a full rush of vertigo went to your head and made it throb. Consequently, you tried not to bend over or move fast. You had to regulate your breathing in hopes it would ease your aching brain. Dealing with anything complicated, like opening a knife, could wait.

But the Goulds were going at it full throttle—no levity, no tolerance. Tents were blowing away in the wind, loose ends snapping at them, striking them on the back of the head or face. Words of despair would get caught in the airstream and waft out, "I don't know if I can go further," and "I feel like shit, this is god-awful."

Borgel, Lewis and I reached White Rock around 7:00 PM. The three of us worked as a well-oiled machine setting up our bivouac and had no problems. We never had problems with each other either. What sense would that make? For example, I'd make some bold statement like, "I was at the first game of the 1988 World Series when the Dodgers swept the Athletics. Kurt Gibson came out of the lockers in the bottom of the 9th, the score was three/two, Athletics ahead, two runners on base. With the Dodgers behind by two, Gibson came to the plate and knocked it out of the park on a three-two pitch, into the right field bleachers about twenty feet from me. That was the greatest event in sports history."

Borgel would laugh and allow me the fun of it all, but Lewis would say, "Nah, the greatest moment in sports history was..." and he would come up with something else. It was the quintessential male bonding experience, the comradery of men. It's a miracle the three of us got along so well. Thank God for that bond—I can easily imagine a different scenario. Then White Rock would have been Hell.

Dick Gordon could've come over to torture us. Dick was a freeloader, not part of the commercial group. Enrique picked him up at *Puente del Incas* and offered him a "piggyback" position with the guides, in return for his help with the "team." Therefore, his services were not outlined specifically, and Enrique, not wanting to expose the imposter, or just not caring, allowed Dick's focus to change from service to making it "to the summit."

The trouble with him was his take-charge attitude that came with strong opinions as to why he couldn't be wrong. His know-it-all attitude earned him no friends at

White Rock. We heard him in a nearby tent, and every time he turned restless in his sleep, Craig or Bill would say sarcastically, "Kind of tough to sleep, huh?"

Bill thought those tents were small until he had to sleep with three people in it, then he understood the sardine analogy. This is what expedition climbing is all about. How much can you take after putting yourself in the worst conditions known to mankind: you can't breathe, it's 20 degrees below zero, you have shitty food, and now you're cramped into a tiny tent.

There's an art to getting your clothes on and off inside the tent. Deciding what to wear in the morning, and which ones you're sleeping in is a big concern. Everyone's gear is in the tent, so you must try and keep it organized. There is no privacy, you're jammed in the tent and can't move without disturbing two other people. Even if someone is hurting or having a god-forsaken sinus problem, you want to have compassion, but it's like "Shut the fuck up and die on your own time! I'm trying to get some sleep here."

But you're probably not sleeping at 18,000 feet. You're just waiting to turn on your other side again. Everything inside the tent is frozen. You want your boots nearby, you pile gear inside your sleeping bag, saving enough room for water bottles, the most precious commodity. Then the wind starts to blow hard, it yowls and shakes the condensation off the inside of the tent onto your face. The rattling starts on the loose skin of the tent, sometimes the wind blows so hard the whole tent is peeled down to the ground as though it was going to blow away.

We woke up from our naps around 8:30 PM and felt much better. Once our tent was pitched, we fell in and laid across each other to sleep for a bit. Lewis complained he pulled a muscle in his back picking up rocks to use as tent anchors. He was hunched over like an old man.

When we arrived at White Rock, Borgel was coughing and spitting up blood. Enrique told him he had pulmonary edema, although he never checked his vital signs. It was just a sore throat from breathing so hard, and he was fine after drinking water. It was okay and he couldn't wait until tomorrow to finally get it done.

Enrique told us to ready our gear. We would be awakened by 5:00 AM if the weather was good, if not good, then 6:00 AM. "You get up. I give you something to eat, and you go."

The next day at exactly "no time" did anybody come to wake us up or give us a complimentary roust or acknowledge our presence in any way. The whole camp got up before us at 6:00 or 7:00 and was under way. They had eaten every scrap of food, every packet of oatmeal, and took another packet for their private stash to eat during the day.

That was a big surprise because by the time we got on our five layers of underwear and pile, and Gore Tex and bib overalls, and were able to pull our boots over our three socks, and get those frozen bastards tied, and put on our liners and two pairs of gloves and mittens, and get our protective gear on our heads and our torches burning, we were the last ones in camp with nothing to eat. It was every man for himself.

I was more upset with myself. I knew better and should have taken precautions against it. What's done is done. Fuck the food, I wasn't hungry anyway, but then we found some packets of cocoa, drank it, and felt nourished enough to race out of there – at a snail's pace. We were behind the last man by about an hour. There is an unnerving fear about being left behind. I didn't like it and neither did Lewis and Borgel.

We were running on a type of nervous energy that's a cross between, "we're never going to catch up," and "I don't belong back here," and "god-damn those guys, we'll show them."

MT. ACONCAGUA

We did show them because we caught up and passed the Gould family and Anil and caught up to Bill: but that wasn't good enough. The challenge was to close the 1,000-foot gap Neil and Trevor put between us by starting their climb at 7:45 with headlamps. Craig and Dick were ahead of them. By the time we caught up to Bill on the *Canaleto*, Neil and Trevor were 400 feet ahead, on the summit.

If we kept our pace, we'd be summiting at 5:00 PM. That was an hour after Enrique said was the cut-off for the last man to summit; but fuck him. Our plan was not easy but within the general guidelines of mountaineering etiquette. Getting our asses "to the summit" is the priority, if the weather holds, and barring any unforeseen accidents. It was 4:00 in the afternoon. We had 400 feet to the top of the 23,320-foot summit of Aconcagua. We could be there in one hour.

Energizer Baby

Somehow Anil got the jump on the Goulds. He's like the Energizer Bunny, he just keeps going and going. We passed him on the slope above the *Independencia Refugio*, where there's an A-frame house, a very little (4 X 6) structure the Argentinian's pass off as the highest permanent building in the world at 21,400 feet. Anil was walking real, real slow, demonstrating the same muscle skills used by Staciak on his way to *Nido*. I didn't believe he was coherent, but to the question, how do you feel? he answered "fine." He didn't want to talk, nor did I.

I wanted to get across the traverse and start climbing up the *Canaleto*, which is like saying, I want my worst nightmare to come true, then double it. There is a perception problem when it comes to the traverse. A "traverse" refers to a path, high up, that extends laterally across the mountain.

Firstly, this traverse cuts across the middle of the *Gran Acarreo* or "Big Haul" as it is justifiably named, and the Big Haul covers the whole Northwest side of the mountain. The "traverse" starts at 21,500 and is covered in ice and hard packed snow, partially hidden in the shadows. The grade of the traverse is not steep, but as you angle around the slow curve towards the *Canaleto* it begins to torture you.

Secondly, you can see the traverse clearly from our camp at *Nido de Condores*. It looks like the trail extends a couple of hundred yards long, not realizing you're looking at it from 6,000 feet away. That is a depth perception issue. This traverse is a monstrous, never-ending ice trail, at least

MT. ACONCAGUA

1,000 linear feet, crossing the mountain with a 6,000-foot drop.

When we got to the traverse, Lewis, Borgel and I stopped to put on our crampons in a clumsy, laborious manner. Bill was about 100 feet ahead of us on the trail. Behind us, we see Anil stumbling like a somnambulist up the path. Out of sight and behind Anil, the 'Swiss Family Robinson' was blowing up.

Enrique, on one of his many trips back and forth from the summit that day, had met with Mother and Daughter Gould on the trail above *Independencia*. They had fallen behind Mr. Gould and King, due to a Dachstein Mitten attack on Mumsy. Enrique observed Mumsy's strange behavior. Mumsy and Nunzie were in last place, bringing up the rear and doing a poor job of it.

Mumsy was having a heck of a time getting her gloves on. She was trying to adjust her mittens and accidentally took off her liners. Then, she couldn't get the thumbs of the liners inserted in her Dachsteins, which are huge woolen mittens, which makes it hard to imagine. "The thumbs were tight, cutting off the circulation, which was the reason she fell so far back;" also hard to imagine.

Sometime later, Mr. Gould and King were walking well ahead of the Gould girls. They had almost made it to the traverse. Enrique passed by them again on his way back to check on what was happening with the girls. He took one look at Mumsy still fighting with her gloves and this time told her the jig was up, and she must go down to White Rock. "It will take too many hours to reach the summit at your pace." he said. "Tents are available at White Rock with your equipment inside. It will be a comfortable place for you to rest until the others get back."

Enrique coddled Mumsy and assured Nunzie her mother would be fine. So, Nunzie walked on to meet up with her dad. Upon hearing the decision regarding his wife, Mr. Gould was not happy with the news. Why should Mumsy have to go down? Another decision had been made without consulting Mr. Gould. "This cannot be!" he exclaimed.

King flipped out over the news about Mom. When Nunzie told him Enrique said Mumsy would be okay by herself, he lost it, yelling "I don't care what Enrique says. Someone has to be with Mumsy."

There ensued an hour-long debate between the three of them over who would go with Mumsy. First, King offered to go down, then Nunzie, amazed at King's selfless attitude, offered to go down. Then Dad started walking down for Mumsy. Then King and Nunzie ran after Dad and

MT. ACONCAGUA

tried to explain their point of view, talking at the same time. What a mess?

They argued away an hour of precious time over who would go with Mumsy. They had become victims of their own false pride, making arguments why somebody should go with Mumsy, but nobody ever going. Hell, Mumsy could have walked off the side of the mountain if Enrique hadn't gone to help her to White Rock.

~

King was a big believer in the buddy system. "Nobody thinks a climber will get hurt until they do—look at Tom Taplin, good thing somebody was with him," King said. "The trail down seems safe, but a person could trip and fall, they can get disoriented and wander off, they can feel in trouble and want to descend or lay down and die. Their decision-making ability is impaired. There might be no food at White Rock," said King, "or fire." That's why King insisted somebody must go back with Mumsy. But who?

As this was happening, Mumsy was taken to White Rock and Enrique was back again at the Gould debate. Nunzie was adamant that King should not have to descend but still held her ground as to herself not going down. The clock was ticking until she conceded that King should accompany Mr. Gould to the summit. (Fat chance of that happening.) Nunzie finally said it, "King, you and Dad were on the original team. You go for it."

She made the selfless decision to descend and made it for a group reason. "It was my choice," she announced with pride. She needed a banner. Raw-Raw!

Enrique accepted Nunzie's decision, turned toward the traverse with Mr. Gould and King, and immediately left them in the dust. That was the bitter end of the road upwards for the Goulds. They were now three hours behind us and another two hours from the summit.

When Nunzie reached White Rock, her mother acted surprised to see her. It was Mumsy's fault she had to return, of course. Mumsy had no business putting herself in danger on summit day, and she flat ruined her daughter's bid for the summit. It was neither fair nor smart. There was nothing left to do about it. Nunzie said she "chewed the bridle" for a bit. She crawled into her sleeping bag and dozed for a few hours dreaming of what might have been, and who ruined it for her.

MT. ACONCAGUA, ARGENTINA (1989)

13.
Anil Makes a Mistake

Enrique now had groups of climbers in twos or threes, spread across the mountain from the summit down to the beginning of the traverse. After leaving camp at White Rock that morning there was no collective pace amongst the climbers, and the mountain became a free for all.

This made it tough for a climber like Anil who liked to walk by himself. Whether he liked to walk by himself, or nobody wanted to walk with him, remains a question. But it put him away from the crowd, and that's where he ended up. I was 150 feet ahead of Anil, and King and Mr. Gould were 150 feet behind him, at the trailhead of the traverse.

You must understand how difficult it is to get your crampons working right at 21,500 feet before you can understand the amount of time it takes to continue the icy traverse. A long time. I may have been 150 feet ahead of Anil when he sat to put on his crampons, but I was completely across the remainder of the traverse and started up the *Canaleta* by the time he finally gave up putting them on.

There is a serious issue of negligence here. Anil had paid for a guide to act as a guide. He sat on a rock for an hour toiling to put crampons on his Bunny Boots which was never going to work in the first place. Crampons are not to be worn on those bulbous, white rubber boots that fit your feet like tugboats.

Never, under any conditions, should you even attempt to wear crampons on Bunny Boots. Period. The sole is too flexible, it can turn and twist, and there's no rim around the sole of the boot to hold and lock the crampon in place, otherwise you walk right out of them. The boot has no rigidity, it's soft and pliable around the ankle, and the boot goes up and down so your foot slides back and forth. All leading to catastrophic results.

Yet Anil said he watched Enrique put the crampons on the night before. Enrique had adjusted them by bending the boot out of the metal clip that normally holds the crampons in place, and tightened it with bolts holding tension from the bottom... and Anil was surprised when they came off? Are you kidding me?

Anil never got the crampons on. His hands were freezing, his fingers were numb, and he didn't want to take

MT. ACONCAGUA

off his gloves to fix the crampon. He decided he didn't need them. "That was my mistake," he later admitted. The climbers who traversed to the *Canaleta* before him had loosened the ice, effectively cutting steps on the path he thought would hold him for the next fifteen or twenty feet. (He didn't know it was 1,000 feet long.). "I was thinking very rationally when I made that decision. My goal was to reach the summit at all costs."

Once Anil started to cross the traverse, he moved carefully, slowly shuffling his feet, picking his steps, and then…both feet slipped from under him like a kid standing on a skateboard.

Poor Anil landed on his butt and began sliding down the 6,000 ft. drop, with a 65 percent grade, known as the *Gran Acarreo*. He had on glasses and was blind without them. He dug with his hands and feet in the snow, but it was too steep. Grabbing for anything to arrest his speed, there was nothing but a billion little rocks everywhere across the wide *Acarreo,* but no flat ground to slow him down.

Anil spotted an outcropping of rocks coming up ahead and thought, "If I could buttress myself on those rocks with my flank, and trap my body against the outcropping, then I could at least slow down." But he heard a horrific crack when he passed the rock, realizing he'd hit his head, and not his flank on the rock. He was hitting his legs, shoulders, hip, back, face, bouncing all over the *Stone Sentinel*, just like a rag doll thrown out the window of a moving car.

Down the mountain he fell, first sliding *hundreds* of feet, then bouncing through the black pyramid of shade made by Aconcagua's peak across the *Asarreo*. Three, four hundred more feet, then back into the sun he tumbled. Once he hit the outcropping with his head, he knew he was going to die. That was the end. When he stopped, he looked the size of a peanut viewed from above. And below, he looked a bloody tangled mess. The only place he didn't break a bone was in his legs, so he was able to walk out with the aid of help.

"It felt so good sliding fast. I'd smashed my head and thought I was already dead. I'd lost my glasses and could no longer see," Anil told Tom Taplin in his book *The Stone Sentinel*.

Obviously, Dr. Anil Patel lost something more than common sense.

The Canaleta

Where were our guides? Most expeditions leave a guide at drag to pick up stragglers, advise late comers, or help anyone who'd gotten sick or fallen. That's the routine—both a good rule to follow and a mandatory one if you're guiding a commercial expedition.

Enrique acted as though he had never heard of such a rule and challenged its efficacy because it got in the way of his going to the summit. Enrique had traditionally been the first one to congratulate the mountaineers as they summited on previous expeditions. He was miffed when he got the relay call that Anil Patel needed help. He, and the other two guides, were going balls out for the summit, and now, "Darn, again, just what I need, another problem," thought Enrique.

The *Canaleta* is the worst trail you could dream up— scree, then boulders, then back to scree. Lewis, Borgel and I finished the traverse and started up the snow field at the base of the *Canaleta* about 900 vertical feet below the summit. We could see Enrique, Pepe, Gustavo, Dick, Trevor, and Neil either on the summit or approaching it. They were 600 feet above us— an hour and a quarter walk at the pace we were going. We were going to make it.

We stopped to rest about twenty yards from one another when we thought we heard something. But the yells were faint. We had no idea who was yelling, or why. There's a bend in the route where the snow field curves into the *Canaleta*, making it impossible to see a climber's progress along the traverse. I had no plans of walking down to look.

We heard more shouts, "Help! Help! Anil has fallen off the mountain! Get help. Get Enrique!"

Now the shit has hit the fan. No more, Mr. Nice guy, something must be done, but where are the rescuers? Anil picked the wrong spot for us to help. Goddamn Enrique better get his butt down here pronto. We were between three hundred to five hundred yards from the accident site. That's two hours of climbing in the wrong direction that couldn't be made up or done again by us mere mortals. It meant going down and essentially quitting.

We yelled up to Bill, Bill hollered up to Neil and Trevor, and we all stopped dead in our tracks to wait for Enrique who had run back up to the summit.

As we were waiting, Borgel said to us, "Hey man, I'm feeling pretty beat. I'm going down with Enrique to help the Doctor." That's about all he had to say. We made sure that's what he wanted to do, but he looked close to being overextended and I might not be doing him any favors by encouraging him. I told him if he didn't summit today, he could summit tomorrow.

Enrique arrived with Gustavo and informed us the climb was over; we must go down. I looked at him and said, "You can forget that. I'm going to the top."

Enrique took off with Borgel and confided to him, "Those two, they don't listen. I don't care. Let them do what they want!"

"Enrique, that's not the way it is at all," said Borgel.

"See, now you argue with me," Enrique sputtered back.

Lewis and I carried on, got off the snow field and took our crampons off. Then we started up the boulder field. It's a slope to the right of the *Caneleta* that comes as advertised, filled with boulders, not rocks or scree, it's just boulders you must climb up and over to get to the top. It was much easier than scree, but with less oxygen it's hard to lift your foot to climb a boulder, so it's Natures last way of testing you. Eight breaths between steps.

Bill was twenty yards up and looked as though he was having a rougher time than us. Who knows? We kept climbing.

Then it started to snow; first a little, then a lot, in light furies, then whirlwinds of snow would touch down here and there so lightly, before they got angrier. A sure sign there's a blizzard brewing. The clouds were rolling up the side of the mountain, drifting in and out. The 'black cloud' popped out from behind the summit and got so big, bigger, then massive. Craig and Dick were coming down fast from the top and wasted no time talking to us. It was over for them.

Bill pointed out we'd be caught in a whiteout, with the snow covering our path, and none of us knowing jack shit about being 23,000 feet up a mountain without a guide in a whiteout. That would be a predicament. We looked down to see our path disappear under a sheet of snow, which left an eerie fright. The same as being left behind.

I headed up the trail, Lewis hung back, Bill went down.

The way I figured; I came to climb the mountain. Hell, anybody can find their way down a mountain. Just follow the contour of the landscape and head that way. I don't need a guide for going down, I just came that way.

I started up because daylight was burning, and I was using it. Besides, it was 400 feet to the summit, I'd only be 100 feet from the top by the time Neil and Trevor came

MT. ACONCAGUA

down, and they'll have Pepe with them. It's going to work out.

Finally, Lewis gave a shout out to me. Lewis said he promised his wife he wouldn't do anything stupid. He says, he said, "Mark, I'm not going any further. It's snowing too hard."

But what I heard was, "Hey Mark, give it up. To hell with it, it's all over. Let's go down."

Right about then I saw a clear spot in the sky, one last ray of hope. I traversed to the middle of the *Canaleta* thinking this storm cloud would pass too, but no – it didn't pass. It got bigger and uglier, and it stared at me. I could see the Devil dancing in the blackness of that cloud, and she showed me my fate. You die if you try to fight this storm. I just needed to see it for myself.

I was extremely disappointed. I had no expectation other than summiting. It was difficult to accept. There's nothing more frustrating than having the weather come fuck up your dream; but there's nothing you can do about it. That was the first time something like that happened to me. My entire life plan was geared on making the summit, and that was not to be.

Scraaatcheeech Kaboom! You must change gears. I changed gears.

Standing top (left to right):

Jason Frank, Andy Frank, Kingdon Gould III, Tom Taplin

Standing bottom (left to right):

Bill English, Daniel Burrieza, Tom Borgel, Gregg Lewis, Mr. Gould (?) Anil Patel, Mark Cornwall, Trevor Byles, Neil Delehey, Greg Stasiak and Mike Milford.

Copyright 1989 © Tom Taplin

MT. ELBRUS, RUSSIA

14.
Get Rid of It

Who would mind if Mt. Elbrus was taken off the list of Seven Summits and Mont Blanc put back on? Could there be a more boring mountain in the world than Elbrus? Does anybody know what it looks like? Have you heard anybody say something good about the climb? I know a guy named Marv who climbed Elbrus. The best he could say was, "It's just a long sludge up the mountain that was a lot harder than I thought it would be."

Everybody is entitled to their opinion, but Dick Bass, the Godfather of Seven Summits, commits only three pages to the climb of Elbrus in his 336-page book on *Seven Summits*. That's less than one percent of the whole book. Bass's account goes something like this:

"We took a rickety aerial tram from 7,500 to 10,000 feet, a more-rickety single chair ski lift to 11,500 and then hiked a moderate slope to 13,300. We spent the night in a metal sheathed hut that looked like a huge Airstream trailer. Left at 4:00 A.M. in the morning, Frank, of course, had a scary outburst on the exposed traverse, then we summited. Morgan

threw up twice on the statue of Lenin, then we came down. Other than that, the entire trip was a drab, dreary pain in the ass, every moment formulated and controlled by restrictions. As a good-bye, Russia shot down Korea's 747, so it was a hassle getting out of the hole."

There you have it, the Mt. Elbrus experience. That's what you miss if replaced by a mountain on the continent of Europe. Elbrus is no more a summit in Europe than Indonesia is on the Australian continent. Nobody knows why Elbrus was chosen to be the highest summit in Europe, except maybe nobody wanted the French to have it.

Mt. Blanc is a 15,781-foot peak in the heart of central Europe, and traditionally everyone agreed it was Europe's highest mountain. Mt. Elbrus, at 18,510 feet, only 2,729 feet higher, is in the heart of the Greater Caucasus Range, the natural border between Europe and Asia. Elbrus is near the Georgian border in Kabardino-Balkaria and Karachay–Cherkessia, Russia, south of the Kama–Mynch Depression. That sounds like the backdrop to Tolstoy's *Cossacks.*

To get to Mount Elbrus from Mont Blanc, head east across Austria, Hungary, and Romania. When you reach Ukraine, bear right around the Black Sea to its extreme eastern shore in Georgia. Then follow the crest of the natural border east along the Greater Caucasus' watershed for about 100 miles, and there you are, on the highest mountain peak in Russia, Asia!

Ivan has thrown a Molotov cocktail into the politic of how and why this mountain was determined to be in the Seven Summits. The fact Mt. Elbrus is in Asia was first discovered and reported in 1730 by Philip Johan von Strahlenberg, one of the most distinguished cartographers in history. He was a Swedish military officer, explorer, and geographer who, after being defeated by the Russians in the Northern War, was exiled to Tobolk for ten years as his punishment. Living in the Caucasus Range during this decade of detention allowed Strahlenberg to study the geography of the region. Upon returning to Stockholm, Sweden he wrote his major treatise *An Historico-Geographical Description*.

The maps in his book of cartography established the natural boundaries between the continents as they are recognized throughout the world today. The eastern boundary of the European continent runs down the Ural Mountains to the Emba River, which flows into the north Caspian Sea. The boundary turns west from the Caspian and runs to the Black Sea along the Kuma-Mynch

Depression, a geological depression caused by the rivers of the same name.

The land mass south of this depression, stretching between the two seas, is Asia. All the Greater Caucasus Mountain Range, including the countries of Georgia and Azerbaijan are entirely on the Asian Continent. One look at a topographical map between Georgia and Russia makes this demarcation the natural choice that places Mt. Elbrus in Asia.

Look it up! I'm not making this stuff up. It's been the boundary between the European and Asian continents since the Russian Tsars first accepted Strahlenberg's postulation based on their own Russian geographers' studies in the mid-18th century. Strahlenberg's postulation is the official Russian definition of the boundary between the two continents presently being taught in textbooks in the USSR. This much authority is enough to convince the sternest Judge in the World Court at the Hague, that Mt. Elbrus is in Asia.

There are no tectonic plates beneath the continents to argue otherwise, nor space photos showing where the continents collided. That means defining the continental line between Europe and Asia is not possible in any scientific manner. It depends on the sources consulted, all with different political agendas. Which candidate do you want to win? It's a formative and artificially abbreviated political decision that involves your life, money, pleasure and in larger part, the satisfaction you want to achieve knowing you climbed Europe's highest mountain.

Sorry Dick Bass, but this finding negates your *Seven Summits*. That's too bad.

Making the Dream

Every mountaineer needs a working knowledge of world geography. It would be difficult to discuss *Seven Summits* without it. The aspiring *Seven Summiteer* should understand why Mt. Elbrus, or Carstensz Pyramid for that matter, were chosen over the traditional highest mountain on the continent. This is particularly true when modern choices replaced historically accepted mountains for no apparent reason.

Mt. Elbrus has no alluring attributes that make it a preferred climb over any other two-day summit in the world. Mont Blanc, on the other hand, is a rock climber's paradise, with handholds in all the right places, on the day-long rock climb to the Hut. Elbrus has nothing to compare to the technical portions of the Mont Blanc climb, easy or difficult, because there are no technical parts on Elbrus, making Elbrus the most boring trudge of all.

Yet Elbrus has twice the death toll of Mont Blanc each year —an average of thirty deaths a year as opposed to fifteen on Mont Blanc. Explain that to someone you love before you climb Elbrus. If a mountaineer is challenging a peak where they could lose their life, they should be damn sure it's the mountain they want to climb, and not one chosen by an elite class with different motives. There's no place in mountaineering for *noblesse oblige*.

A brief look of how the *Seven Summits* came to be exposes the motive of certain climbers, namely Reinhold Messner, and in this case Dick Bass, who have managed to re-define for all other climbers what their mountain choices should be.

In 1956, the first person to be acknowledged for climbing to the top of five continents was William D. Hackett. His summits included Mont Blanc (not Elbrus), Kosciuzko (not Carstensz Pyramid), McKinley, Aconcagua, Kilimanjaro, but no Mt. Everest or Vinson Massif.

In 1970, Naomi Umemura was celebrated as the first person to climb five bigger summits which included Mont Blanc (not Elbrus), McKinley, Aconcagua, Kilimanjaro, and Everest, but no Kosciuzko or Vinson.

MT. ELBRUS

In 1978, Reinhold Messner was celebrated as the first person to climb six of his *Seven Summits* which included Carstensz Pyramid, Aconcagua, Mt. McKinley, Kilimanjaro, and Mt. Everest. Messner determined for himself, much to the chagrin of others, that Carstensz Pyramid was the highest peak in Australia.

But to satisfy his critics, and the rest of the world's opinion that Carstensz did not satisfy the geographic definition of Australia, Messner condescended and climbed Mt. Kosciuszko in 1983. That was the same year Dick Bass was attempting to climb all his seven summits in one year, including Kosciuszko, not Carstensz.

In 1978, with Messner's unquestioned success in reshaping the continent of Australia by declaring Carstensz Pyramid the highest mountain on the submerged continental shelf, apropos of nothing, he decided he could reshape the border between Asia and Europe and declared Mt. Elbrus was the highest peak in Europe.

This is where you've got to ask, "Why?" So they could climb 2,729 feet higher?

This recalculation of Europe's and Russia's highest summit was accepted by other members in Messner's elite mountaineering community for several practical reasons.

<u>The first being they</u> are world-class climbers from Europe, all too familiar with the hordes of want-to-be climbers that flood the Alps every season.

<u>And</u> those hordes come by the thousands to invade what Messner, and other elites, feel is their native land. <u>This</u> interferes with their indigenous right to spend climbing time in the Alps.

Mt. Elbrus manages to put the highest summit in Europe, in communist Russia, exactly where the elites want it. That's the foundation of the so-called Messner list, to get the hordes out of the Alps. Send them to Siberia. Well, the Caucasus anyway...

Why did Dick Bass and Frank Wells climb Mt. Elbrus, and not Mont Blanc in 1983? A matter of convenience. Expeditions are difficult to plan and planning seven of them over a year's time is nearly impossible. Elbrus fell into their schedule perfectly because it was easy to reach from Kilimanjaro's Africa. Frank Wells, who attempted Mt. Elbrus twenty years before, was hit by altitude sickness on the climb and couldn't tie his shoelaces at 10,000 feet. He wanted a re-do. Bass wanted seven summits in a year. Mt. Elbrus was a quick knock-off they could accomplish immediately after their Kilimanjaro climb. As the *Seven*

MT. ELBRUS

Summits book puts it, it was up, down, three pages, and they were out.

They also had resources to provide the necessary diplomatic, financial, and business connections to get things done in Russia without a hitch. They were looking for speed. As their book indicates, they had better mountains to climb. So much for a "true mountaineer's objective."

Why would I take so much time and trouble to point out God did not create the Seven Summits, Messner and Bass did? There is something insidious about Bass's quest that can fool the average lover of mountains. Because Bass was an amateur who succeeded at his dream, it leads every other armchair mountaineer to believe they can do the same thing. Bass made it look easy.

But making it look easy is a double-edged sword. The underdog inspiration of a previously untrained amateur with dogged determination is great, but to forget his dream was fueled by nothing less than a billion dollars of Dick's personal resources would be fanciful.

His finances don't undermine his physical achievement of climbing the mountains, but for the average untrained amateur to attempt a seven-summit quest without Dick's dough, would find it hard to duplicate. How much could you pay for the privilege of climbing Mt. Everest —twice!

You want to get the most bang for your buck. Dick Bass inherited a fortune from his oil tycoon Dad and made it a bigger fortune. More power to him. Forbes put his present worth above $5 billion. But neither he, nor Messner, nor any of their elitist bullshit is going to define my Seven Summits. Especially since their list was chosen according to their personal agendas, and quite frankly, they are both wrong. So *Noblesse oblige that, motherfuckers.*

That's the lesson. There's sweat on every dollar I've earned. I'm not spending a dime on someone else's expensive pipe dream. I've always wanted to create my own life but getting started in the business world isn't easy when your father isn't a Texas oil tycoon.

MT. BLANC, FRANCE (1992, 1994, 1999)

15.
A Challenge to Climb

Time and money are all it takes. I returned three times to Chamonix, France, and to Zermatt, Switzerland to climb Mont Blanc and the Matterhorn in the same trip. I went first in 1992, then again in 1994, and finally summited both peaks in 1999. That was a decade quest from the time I met Valentin Trenev, the *Bulgarian Hulk,* in 1989, to my standing on the Matterhorn's summit with him ten years later, on my third try.

In the words of Messner and Morrow, "If you are looking for the more challenging climb," then forget the ugly sludge up Elbrus in Russia and acquaint yourself with two of the more iconic mounts in the heart of Alpine country: Western Civilization's time-honored highest mountain in Europe, Mt. Blanc, and the "Crown Jewel of the Alps," the Matterhorn.

You will be sorely disappointed with your Alpine adventure if you don't believe summitting Mont Blanc, then the Matterhorn will make you feel like a rockstar. They are only forty miles apart. This is where you separate yourself from the hordes of client adventurers. By showing you think for yourself, you become wiser in the process. Guaranteed!

It doesn't work the other way around. Climbing Mt. Elbrus in Russia will not make you feel as good. If you didn't substitute the Mont Blanc/Matterhorn climb for the Elbrus climb, you'd feel like you'd been cheated. Like you did exactly what Messner wanted you to do, you've made yourself a victim. Like you didn't read Bass's book about pissing on Lenin's head. Bass will forgive you for *not* climbing Elbrus if you forgive his fateful error in climbing it. Who do you answer to? You will *not* be getting your bang for the buck by climbing Mt. Elbrus.

Queuing up the Matterhorn

What does it mean to climb *Seven Summits* anyway? What are you trying to get out of life? Who are you? Are you courageous? Can you handle fear? Will you quit because of the pain, or because you have a girlfriend, or wife and kid back home? A lot of climbers quit. Most of them quit when death stares them in the face. They get afraid of losing something. Losing what? Losing your life by being smashed on the rocks below? What the hell are you afraid of? Are you fucking scared?

MT. BLANC

I heard this kind of talk when I was standing at the bottom of the ice wall, 40 feet below the summit of Matterhorn. There is only one fixed rope going to the top. Climbers line up single file along a narrow ridge to wait their turn. The ledge you queue up on falls off 3,000 feet on both sides. On the north side, you can slide to your death down the North Face, like it was the autobahn. On the south side, you can fall thousands of feet before you hit the rocks.

The goddamned Alpinists are pushing and shoving to crowd you out, intimidate you to the back of the line. You elbow them back, standing broader in the shoulders to keep them from passing. Climbers in front and behind are turning back to quit. They came all this way and are now quitting.

The summit is right up this fixed line. Aren't they prepared? Haven't they thought this challenge through? Didn't they work out to build muscles in their shoulders and lats specifically to climb this rope up this ice wall, pulling and digging your crampons to push your gluteus maximus up the summit?

It's a fact that if you slip, lose your grip, dangle and fall, or are reckless, you will die. But who is going to do that? This is not where people get killed. They get killed on the descent, like the accident Valentin says he was privy to.

He was taking a break and entered a conversation with a father and teenage son who were descending. Both were ecstatic about their summit climb. The rocks they were resting on were safe, it was sunny, and nobody was roped up. Two minutes after they parted company the boy came running back screaming that his father had fallen off the mountain. There was nothing Val could do. There was nothing anyone could do now.

We're standing below the summit when Val decides he needs to give me a pep talk. We're facing a psychological hurdle that needs to be addressed because he sees others choosing to quit and somehow that applies to me, and we can't have that.

Val hates the mountain. He's an alpinist, so the mountain is our enemy, trying to kill us. We must move quickly to evade death. Therefore, he believes in yelling in a person's face, shouting insults to make him/her mad, humiliating them, trying to make them blind with anger. Val thinks this will create the right energy necessary to attack the mountain. That's what he calls inspiration. Maybe that's what he was taught in Bulgaria. I never asked, nor cared, and I didn't want any of it.

He was in the middle of calling me a god-damn fucking pussy if I didn't...

"What the fuck are you talking about?" I said slowly so he could hear each syllable. "I have no idea what you're talking about. Shut the fuck up before I plant my fist so far in your face, I can't pull it out."

I'd made my decision long ago.

I didn't really say the part about planting my fist in his face, but that's the anger he wanted me to feel—enraged and then apply that force to the climb. But I didn't have time to think such a stupid thought. That's not why I come to the mountains. I'm the exact opposite when faced with danger, or otherwise panicky situations. I get calm and that helps me determine how to deal with the situation.

In this case, it was grab the rope and climb the hell up that ice wall, pulling with my arms, pushing with my crampons, just as I planned. I had no time for Val's distracting anger techniques.

I've got nothing against encouraging words. The style I respond to best was personified by Phil Penny, my guide on Mt. Cook in New Zealand. Maybe it was his accent, but he would say things like, "Well, Mark, we're getting close. Those last twelve pitches were tough. I know I'm tired. But here's the deal, now it's going to get tougher, front-pointing up this ice wall isn't easy, but the summits right there. I bet you'd be disappointed if you got back to Santa Barbara and didn't finish it off?"

Who could take offense to that? "You goddamn right, Red Rider."

Mont Blanc is a Challenge?

Compared to what? Elbrus? Mont Blanc is where you might find three, or even four tourists being pulled up the mountain by their French guide. I'm not kidding. I saw a guide literally pulling a pudgy tourist up the moderately easy rock climb to the Gouter Hut. The guide had a pathetic look on his face, disgusted with his chore. They'll pull anything up the mountain for $500.00. They made it to the Hut though, but next time the tourist should hire an extra guide to push from the bottom.

The climb in the morning to the summit from the Gouter Hut is on glaciered ice. It is a long, hard arc up the ridge, kind of like walking up a glaciered marshmallow. But watch out— Mont Blanc's glacier ice has many crevasses and conditions include rockslides and avalanches. Plus, there are plenty of climbers on the trail, making for a long procession of headlamps, so the fissures in the ice are usually well marked.

MT. BLANC

The first time I attempted to climb Mont Blanc was in 1992, when I was climbing solo. There were hundreds of people in front of me and hundreds behind. But the weather got so foggy I couldn't see the top of my boots. The hordes, climbing single file on ropes, came to a crevasse which I may, or may not have, been able to run and jump over if I really tried. It was dark and looked eerie with the light of the headlamps catching the mouth of the opening, shining inside, giving me a strobe light view of the danger. It spoke to me.

I stepped aside and watched the climbers manage to jump over the width of the black hole with the aid of others. It was always close, and they were roped up. They managed this maneuver tied together in groups of three to four, going one at a time. The problem was I had no one to help me. They had paid good money for guides to watch out for their safety, not mine. It was every man for himself.

I am the one who does not fall into the crevasse. Therefore, I chose not to attempt it. It would have been sheer stupidity. I could envision my miscalculation, my crampon snarled on the ice, or the ledge cracking under the weight of my jump. There would be no one to save me, to help me not slide down the side as I was stabbing the ice with my axe to save my life like Tom Taplin. I was not prepared for this. Mont Blanc was my training ground for acclimatization to climb the Matterhorn, not to be lost in the bottom of a crevasse.

I turned around and started down. Soon I was alone on my descent, the hordes had passed. The icy mist thickened, and I couldn't see my hand in front of my face. Pounding the tip of my axe on the glacier's surface, I slowly felt my way down the slope. The point of my axe suddenly broke through the ice, going a foot deep in the snow, right in front of me. That means don't take another step!

I'd come upon a snow bridge covering a fissure in the glacier. Or perhaps I was on the edge of a crevasse. I poked to the left and right and got the same result. I stepped back in my same tracks, stopped, and gave it some thought. My only choices were to follow my steps back, which was impossible due to darkness and mist, or wait for the fog to clear, or daylight to arrive, because I couldn't see a thing. It was a whiteout. Trying to move from my position could only worsen the danger without being able to see the layout of the land.

Standing in that position, alone, in silence, trapped in one spot with no idea which way to turn, gave me a lonely sensation. I waited bundled up against the cold, thinking, so this is how people disappear off the mountain.

MT. BLANC

The vapor mist engulfed me; ice crystals formed on my sleeves and gloves trying to freeze over me. I pulled my balaclava over my nose. If things got worse, I had a forty-below sleeping bag stuffed in my rucksack.

Then as fast as it had happened, the vapor disappeared, and I was free to move again. Within seconds the sky parted, and the fog and mist were gone. I saw stars twinkling above, followed them to the right, and there was the rock ledge I didn't want to fall over. Followed them left and, what the hell? About a hundred yards away was the silhouette of the Gouter Hut with a lamp post burning brightly. I couldn't believe my eyes. Had my descent bore two degrees west I would have run straight into the Hut and been drinking tea for the last hour instead of standing in the cold.

The lesson was, always climb with a partner, and don't underestimate Mont Blanc. Mont Blanc has crevasses; Mt. Elbrus does not.

So why is Elbrus more challenging?

MT. MATTERHORN, SWITZERLAND
(1992, 1994, 1999)
16.
Third Times the Charm

That first trip to Mont Blanc and the Matterhorn in 1992 was a bust. After my solo defeat on Mont Blanc, I continued to Zermatt to try the Matterhorn. Unfortunately, my climbing plans were foiled by arriving too late in the season. You would have thought I learned my lesson before I did it again in '94. But that's how much you want to avoid the hordes. I didn't leave it to luck the third time, we climbed in mid-season on the 1st of August in 1999.

Valentin was supposed to guide me in '92, but he was having problems with his immigration status into the U.S. Waiting for him cost me a couple of days, which counts plenty when trying to hire a Swiss guide at the end of August. I scoured Zermatt to track one down, but in addition to the guides being sick of climbing the Matterhorn by September, they also want to test your skills before they risk their life to guide you. I swear, you'd think the Swiss guides hated the mountain that fed them.

MT. MATTERHORN

Why would I cast the Matterhorn in a cloak of death? The mountain's shape as a horn in the air may be an alluring attraction, but still, it ain't no thrill ride at Disneyland. Perhaps the familiar image of the 1/100 scale replica of the Matterhorn at Disneyland (147 feet high) lulls climbers into a false sense of security because it's a theme-park joyride. That might help explain the mountain's history of over 500 deaths, with the present annual death toll on the Matterhorn at twelve.

Let's face it, one reason for participating in high altitude climbing is to challenge death. There's a side to climbing that's like Formula 1. Everybody is waiting for the crash, hoping it doesn't happen, but drawn to the sport because it does. That's why mountain climbing is considered a sport.

Far from the image of Mickey Mouse on a bobsled, the Matterhorn is the shape of a finely greased gun, like a German Luger, with its barrel aimed directly at the sun during day, and the moon at night. You don't climb the Matterhorn; you shoot it up. If you don't shoot for the top, either the weather will stop you, or you'll be trampled by the hordes trying to get ahead of you. This is Alpine climbing at its best.

Matterhorn '94

By trying to avoid the hordes of summer in August '94, the weather got us in September. However, we had other hitches in our rope. Because we were trying to climb three on a rope we were moving like molasses. Valentin led the climb, a Thai National named Peter was in the middle, and then me. The rope was making the climb harder than without it. We attempted to put enough slack in the line so we could each climb freely, but the slack was getting snared on rocks, and we were pulling on it constantly. It was tiring.

The Matterhorn can test your rock-climbing skills. There are some tough pitches on the way up, and the first snow at the end of August had just ended the normal season three days earlier. But there we were, just starting up the mountain. Fresh snow made foot holds slippery and our hand holds icy. And because your fingers can't feel the rock with your gloves on, we took them off—so our fingers froze too.

We quit the rope. I don't know what the problem was. Perhaps Valentin wasn't finding the path most used along the Hornli Ridge Route. I suspect he chose a path shorter in length, but steeper and more exposed. I just followed him. The other concern was Peter. He was an excellent rock climber in places like Yosemite or Joshua Tree, but he was slight by nature and not acclimatizing. He was having a heck of a time climbing the rock face of the Matterhorn with his crampons on. He was out of his element.

    I felt sorry for him. Peter was built for tropical weather, lots of heat and humidity. I traveled with Peter to Thailand that same Christmas. We went to Phi-Phi Island where in boiling 129 degrees heat he was scampering up 5.8 rock faces and laughing at it. In the Matterhorn cold he looked encumbered by his oversize jacket and mitten. I couldn't recognize any semblance of the man.

    Not far below the Solvay Hut at 13,133 feet, crisis began to seep from the cracks of the Matterhorn like an alien. I'd never seen it before, but fortunately Val had. At the point the crisis occurred we were traversing the rock slope on a moderate but exposed level; exposed, as in a 2,000 foot drop, but the path was wide enough to pass. Peter was lagging behind me. One thing great about having someone slower than you on the team is you get to rest. This made Val extremely unhappy because it was getting late in the day, and the weather was changing. Black clouds arose on the horizon.

We stopped. Val brushed pass me to see what was wrong with Peter. Peter was leaning back against the rocks as Val started giving him inspiration—calling him the worst of names for his failure to be strong. Peter was not responding. I went back to look at him myself. Peter had been walking unconsciously. His eye lids were fluttering, and his eyeballs began rolling to the back of his head. Val looked at me gravely concerned. He grabbed Peter by the front of his jacket and began to shake him violently.

We wore helmets for protection from falling rocks. But Val was shaking Peter so hard his head was hitting against the stones. He slapped him. He grabbed him around the torso heaving him up and down, squeezing him to force his breathing, igniting his blood flow. One thing was for sure: Nobody was going to die on this mountain under Val's watch. He would do whatever it took, and he did.

Peter came around, barely. Val stripped him of his gear and carried him to Solvay Hut. No easy feat given Solvay hut is built on the edge of nothing, just teetering on the rock face. Its door opens out over the abyss so you can look down the rock precipice to the buried rocks below. You must grab the corner of the hut structure and swing your body out, and over the thousand-foot drop, to get in or out.

MT. MATTERHORN

Once inside, Val buried Peter in his sleeping bag and immediately lit the propane to melt ice for tea. Peter remained unconscious inside his bag. Val massaged Peter's body while forcing him to drink tea. All things wet were hung to dry. This included Val stretching the rope back and forth across the eves to straighten the kinks, assuring its strength for tomorrow.

We were caught in a snowstorm, no doubt about it. There was nothing to do but wait and enjoy the amenities of this tiny wood shelter. The Swiss built it to commemorate the 50th anniversary of Whymper's first ascent in 1865, when four of the seven summiteers were killed on the descent. (Some say the rope was cut to save the remaining three climbers' lives.) Solvay Hut was doing what it was built for: saving lives. As Peter slept, Val explained what he knew of Peter's symptoms. The rolling back of the eyes was the last thing you saw before death.

Val finally got through on the red phone installed in Solvay Hut to alert authorities of any emergencies. I was thinking of the thousands of climbers streaming over the Matterhorn who never saw the inside of Solvay Hut. They should feel good about that. It's far enough off the normal route to the summit, and too high up for day trippers. The normal course is to pass by, see it at a distance, and be glad you didn't have to use it. I couldn't help but think; was this a reflection on us?

Peter had been sleeping for hours when suddenly, and with great gusto, he leaps up from his bag at the waist and yells:

"To the summit!"

It's a miracle, he's cured!

Descent into Death

We weren't going anywhere. We were told by the authorities on the phone that there was no chance of rescue under these storm conditions. That kind of news puts a dagger to your throat. We had only one option. The weather report said there would be a break in the storm the next morning, or if not then, the next morning after that. That would give us the opportunity to make a descent. It also meant we had to climb down the Matterhorn unroped to make our best effort to beat the incoming storm.

The 'incoming storm' is not something you can set your watch to. The mountain makes its own weather and if it wants to kill you it will, just like it does to 12 others every season. The facts were, the Hornli Hut was presently closed for the season. That's the main hut responsible for providing food and shelters for all climbers on the

Matterhorn. The season was over, *nicht mehr, kaput,* which means—by climbing this late in the year, we were actually daring the mountain to take our lives. Had we only known?

For starters, there was no one else on the mountain. The weather was below freezing, and the snow got blustery as a precatory sign of the blizzard's coming. The Matterhorn is made of rock, and every nook and cranny you could lay a hand on was covered in ice or snow. Everything was slippery and wet, you couldn't use gloves on your fingers for fear of losing the feeling for your grip, but at the same time your fingers become numb and potentially frostbitten, making each handhold feel more desperate than the last.

The decision was made; we were going to descend the mountain in the morning. But repelling down with three people wasn't working. Whether it was lack of expertise or otherwise, we were moving too slow. Our only chance for survival was to un-rope and go for it. It was the true definition of "every man for himself."

By the time we started in the morning, we could see the grim reaper on the horizon, a lethal black cloud staring at you. Our mission was clear, we run down the mountain as fast as we can go because otherwise, we're fucked. Good luck, mate!

There was a time when I believed my chances of living were 50/50. 50 percent is pretty dangerous when it's 'life' we're talking about. It was no longer a hypothetical question you ponder in a daydream.

I was living the dream, and it sucked. I either die on the mountain or manage to get off it, and there was only one way to get off —keep moving down the 13,000-foot face of the Matterhorn. As I was crawling down that rock it always felt like I was just one slip away from a 1,000-foot drop before death.

I would work to get one spike of a crampon nudged into a tiny crack or ledge, then pray to God that front fang, jetting out from the front of my boot, would hold one second so I could kick around my other boot to try and find another fang hold for that boot. A search operation of the smallest degree. Every projection on the wall looked minuscule. And this went on for at least two hours, maybe more. I lost my sense of time. Sometimes I would feel exhilarated, but mostly not.

I was stuck eyeball to eyeball with the Matterhorn, clinging to a thin slice of ledge, the wind throwing stinging nettles in my face, my fingertips black, blue, and bleeding. I couldn't find any protrusion below me to place a single fang on my crampon. I could think of only two things.

MT. MATTERHORN

First, I wished for a red button to push and KAZAM, I would be home safe and sound. I would never ever go mountain climbing again. I really wanted that red button. I could push it and be instantly switched to another scene, like in a movie; or like changing the channels on a television set. I'd go directly to *Hee Haw*.

Second, I wondered what would happen if I did fall? I looked down 1,000 feet at the rocks I would fall on and figured I'd hit the brown rocks covered in snow directly below me first, then bounce down that rocky slope, sliding further until I got hung-up on a rock or smashed or maybe just bounce into a snow field.

It could be worse—I could live, then have to lie there and suffer with all my broken bones and no chance of rescue. That was not my imagination, it was a probability. Trust me, you become a damn good rock climber under those conditions, but quick.

About ten feet from the ground, I jumped off into a pool of powder snow and landed waist high in a snow drift against the mountain. Peter took a picture of me with a happy grin. I'm saying, "I'm getting too old for this shit!" I was forty-four.

Of course, I wasn't too old for that shit. In fact, it would be a cold day in hell before I ever said, "I didn't summit the Matterhorn." Who knows why some mountains get into your head and you can't let it go? I had a vision of who I wanted to be in life, and it was a man who climbed to the summit of the Matterhorn. That was one defeat I could not live with, and as I rationalized so many times in my life, how bad could it be anyway? Next time I'll go in mid-season, just like everybody else, to give myself a fair chance.

This idea was augmented a couple of years later when Val took Peter up the Matterhorn wearing shorts in July. I don't believe that of course, Val is too cautious. But I got the picture; I could see skinny Peter in running shorts wearing only light rock-climbing shoes, his black ponytail flying, while doing his victory dance.

"To the summit."

Val told me, when they were standing at the fixed rope of the Matterhorn, Peter let out a scream like a banshee before he grabbed the rope and zipped up the wall. That Peter was quite a character. He ran off to Peru with a girlfriend and I never saw him again.

Matterhorn '99

As for me, Val and I were successful with Mont Blanc and the Matterhorn in 1999, which meant I never had to go to Zermatt again. It seems all great things in mountaineering come with equal parts pain. My climb up the Hornli Ridge to the summit was not exactly a summer's dream. Because of our continuous push, starting at 2:00 in the morning to beat the rush, I never had a moment to adjust my gloves, or massage blood into my fingers at the right time. Not a single second.

We stayed ahead of the hordes until the summit, and that earned me a horrible case of frostbite on the three middle fingers of both hands, particularly the right. I used that hand to steady myself along an ice wall with a foot wide path and nothing but air to the left. The doctor in Zermatt told me I would lose the three tips of my fingers, down to the first knuckle.

That would be the day. I worked them in hot, cold, hot, cold water, stretching and cramping them all day for a month. They came back, but I have no fingerprints on those fingers, (all the better for a life of crime) and the residual effects of frostbite are permanent, and painful when in the cold. When climbing Kilimanjaro the following year, the distinctive burn of frostbite assailed me above 16,000 feet. Like someone hammering a nail in the tip of my finger.

A girlfriend of Val's saw a photo of me smiling, while holding up my black, blistered fingers at the doctor's office in Zermatt. She couldn't understand how I could be happy. I told her, "The satisfaction of the climb outweighed the pain. It meant a lot to me."

MT. MATTERHORN

I'm getting too old for this shit!

"To the summit!"

Valentin inside Solvay Hut

MT. MATTERHORN

TOP OF THE MATTERHORN

The price I paid

MT. COOK, NEW ZEALAND (1997)
17.
Phil Makes the Call

How much do you think it cost for three trips to France and Switzerland? I'm an armchair mountaineer, not a billionaire, and at my present age, my mountain climbing days are in the final stages before I takeoff to never, never land.

The fact I've had a couple of hip replacements, a pacemaker, back surgery, a spinal cord stimulator, nearly died of pneumonia and suffered a stroke in 2015, hasn't helped matters, but I still got game. (At least, that's what my wife says.) So, with life getting in the way of climbing, and one mountain more to climb, I don't have time for do-overs. It's hard enough to get it done once.

Choosing to climb a mountain in the South Pacific with two names nobody can pronounce and located in in a place I don't want to go, makes me uncomfortable. I don't care if most geographers are saying Mount Jayawijaya aka Punkat Jaya aka Carstensz Pyramid, on the island of New Guinea, is the highest mountain in Australia because it's

MT. COOK

part of a larger sub-continent submerged under the South Pacific Ocean called the "Oceania Continent."

All I know is the Oceania Continent includes the islands of Australia, New Guinea, all of Indonesia, Micronesia, but most importantly, the islands of New Zealand, where the Southern Alps are located. In the Southern Alps region, it's called "Australasia," and the highest mountain is "Mt. Cook."

The "Southern Alps" is a Region of New Zealand as beautiful as the name implies. A world of spiraled peaks reigning over a sea of glaciers. There's no place on earth that can rival its abundance of mountain peaks, and it's as far away as you can go in the South Pacific.

It's an American dream! The Aoraki/Mount Cook National Park has 19 peaks over 3,000 meters (10,000 feet) and is covered 40 percent in glaciers; including the 16.7-mile trek up the Tasman Glacier leading directly to Mt. Cook—the highest mountain Down Under at 12,218 feet. The 16.7-mile trek to the Hut is optional, so we opted for a helicopter ride out to begin the climb with my daughter.

It was 6:00 in the morning when Phil pulled in front of the B&B where we were staying. I watched him through the window in the driving rain and wondered what he thought of us. He was driving a VW Camper and sported long blond hair that made him look like a hippy—but an athletic hippy. Not that it mattered. I had curly brown locks down my back when I was 24, but now I'm 47. I used to be married to Aurora's mother, Diana, and now I have Aurora Maxine with me. She's 20 years old. I brought her for good luck...and love. After all, it was Christmas.

Being a father, my first concern upon seeing the athletic blond-haired 28-year-old mountain climber was whether Phil was married. He was, which relieved the sexual tension going on in my brain between guide and daughter. You never know what you'll get when signing up for an international adventure. Sometimes it's great, other times you roll with the punches. But I won the lotto with Phil Penny.

This man measured the indeterminable South Island weather and came up with a plan that made the whole Christmas climb possible. We were forced to climb through the eye of the storm. We had no other choice.

Making the decision to climb Mt. Cook while a storm passed overhead did not come easily. That's the first thing you learn about climbing in New Zealand, you pay attention to the prevailing weather *signs*. It's fundamental to New Zealand climbing.

MT. COOK

We arrived on the South Island in the heart of summer, six days before Christmas. It had been raining on and off, and then on, and then a steady downpour continued all that night and the next. Aurora, Phil and I were busy that first day running around to get more information. Driving from the Hermitage Hotel, we went to the Fish and Game, the Forestry, the head of the Aoraki National Park Weather Dept., the airport, and the Hermitage bar, to get all known data on the climate over Mt. Cook. The data was all the same: stormy weather for days. Not good.

What kind of data were we gathering? Well, Phil was doing the gathering. But we were studying weather maps which look like someone's doodles. Starting with a large oblong circle, you doodle smaller circles inside the bigger circles, each one a little smaller than the last, until you get down to the "eye of the storm" (that part in the middle of the map with no circles in it); then calculate when that smallest circle with no circles in it, passes directly over Mt. Cook. Then we calculate how long the 'eye' will be open. By we, I mean Phil. Who knew it would be sunny inside that smallest circle?

When it stopped raining, we took the map outside and lined it up with Mt. Cook, which could be seen 18 miles away. It looked like the sky was parting above it. The torrential rain had stopped, and you could see a thin ray of light shining on Mt. Cook. The eye was crossing over it right now.

Phil made the decision, "time to go!" We had arranged for the helicopter so there was nothing more to do but jump in and copter out to the Hut. Phil had compared the circular lines on the weather map with those from the last couple of days and was confident we had 24 hours to complete the climb. The window for Mt. Cook was for the next 24 hours, then would close again.

That was a great call! It gave us 24 hours to try and fulfill my dream of climbing the *Seven Summits*. That's what was at stake: a quest of a lifetime. Wouldn't it be sad if someone told me I climbed the wrong mountain? That to climb the *Seven Summits* mandates I would have to climb Mount Jayawijaya aka Punkat Jaya aka Carstensz Pyramid in New Guinea instead of Mt. Aoraki aka Mount Cook in New Zealand? I don't think so. That is, unless you are a Messner who thinks you must do as you're told and follow his rules.

The Boys Go Bottomless

We whirly birded up the Tasman Glacier to the Hut where Aurora was going to sleep and watch us climb. She could remain warm and cozy as she watched her 47-year-old father climb the white mountain Down Under. There was a telescope at the hut to help her view us on the summit.

It would take us two days, that day and the next, to climb Mt. Cook. Aurora had no desire to climb. And it was too technical for her to start now, proving mountain climbing does not run with the genes. She was happy to watch through the scope and read. You boys have fun!

After the chopper dropped us at the Hut, we stashed Aurora and her gear inside, then took off for base camp which we hoped to establish by evening. We dropped Aurora off at 12:30 and began the climb up the Linda Glacier. It's a long haul. We were two dots in a giant bowl of snow, with the threat of avalanches looming on both sides of the valley ahead. The storm held in abeyance as we climbed up the glacier. I was living the dream, and like so many other mountain experiences it was by the seat of my pants.

Aurora was living the adventure with me, only from the hut, which had a fabulous sound system cranking out "hip hop," her brand of music at the time. The Hut lies a few miles from the avalanches of this Alpine Region. And this region is much better than its counterpart in the Northern Hemisphere called the European Continent. There are no hordes getting in your way down here. This was the height of the climbing season between November and February, with the whole world on vacation, and Aurora was the only guest at the Hut. And we were the only two climbers on the mountain.

That was due to the weather, of course. Phil was the only guide to figure out this window of opportunity existed. We had checked for reports on the hour, reading every doodled printout of the storm for days. We only had five days, the limit of Phil's contractual duties. I couldn't wait around in the rain forever, and there sure as heck was no do-over. Come back next season! Not a chance.

And now, here we are, at the foot of Mt. Cook, 12,218 feet, on a sunny day. One of the *Seven Summits*. That's why Phil gets paid the big bucks. We chanced our lives on the fact it would stay cloudless until we left the next day. Phil called it mighty close.

MT. COOK

We trekked up Linda Glacier until it horseshoed at the bottom of Mt. Cook, creating a huge basin. We hiked for hours to find a protected spot high enough up, but far enough away from the avalanches. We finally made camp at the foot of a rolling hill, on the Northside of the summit. It was protected from avalanches because they were falling on the other side of the glacier, a half mile from our base camp.

Phil had a tent with no bottom so when you were sleeping in your bag you could roll over and take a leak in the middle of the night. This was the first time I'd ever seen a no bottom tent. Phil said it made his pack lighter and was a smart way of addressing what is foremost on a climber's mind, taking a piss at night. I felt the need to go that night but couldn't get the hang of peeing outside my sleeping bag while lying down. I couldn't coordinate the effort of getting past two zippers, then pissing far enough away from my bag so as not to make a mess. I decided to get up anyway.

When I did, the midnight sky had tripled the ante of stars. The universe was filled with inspiring stars, billions of stars, in constellations shooting into the milky way, tiny pinholes of stars in the galaxies orbiting the sun, in the guise of satellites and jet planes, sputnik stars coming from black holes. So many stars, it made me dizzy.

I went back into the floorless tent and snuggled into my bag, which now lies directly on the ice of the moraine. I woke up Phil, of course, climbing over his head to get to my bag.

"Hey Phil," I whispered to him. "Maybe you should take both ends of the tent off, make it more like a pup tent? We'd both have views of the stars, and you'd lighten your load some more?"

"Yeah," he said, "I'll wait until it gets balmier. It's still below 0 right now."

"Is that Celsius or Fahrenheit?"

"Celsius. Fahrenheit doesn't mean much down here," said Phil.

"Well, it means a difference of 32 degrees to me," I said.

"Sorry Mark, the rest of the world couldn't learn Fahrenheit so you could understand the temperature. Same problem with kilos, eh? Or how about heights? How are you at converting meters?" retorted Phil.

"Meters? I multiply the number of meters by 3.28 feet. For kilometers to miles, I use the conversion rate of 2.2. So I halve the kilometers, then I take a quarter of the half and add them together for the number of miles. Anything else you want to know?

"Yeah, would you like to know what time it is?" said Phil.

"An hour and a half until we get up?" I observed.

"It's 12:30 at night. The universal time. We've been here 12 hours, with 12 to go."

"Shall we sleep for an hour and a half?"

"Sounds heavenly."

We got up at 2:00 a.m. Conditions were frozen—the safest way to travel is at night. It was dark enough to require headlamps, but light enough to see an outline of Mt. Cook's North/West Summit Ridge. The summit is atop an ice cap just beyond the ridge.

But that outline of the ridge is a far stretch from our base camp. And by 'far stretch' I'm talking about a 5,500-foot gain from our base camp to the summit. It starts by trudging across the basin through the snow onto the Shelf. Then we rock climb up the walls of the Shelf, 7 pitches, to the top of the ridge; then up the 65 percent grade of ice to the summit. Easy Peazy…

A Bad Count

We hiked across the basin for two miles before we were free of avalanche danger. It's not unusual for an avalanche to break off high in the alley and leave its trail across the path you walked on earlier. When we came back that afternoon, we saw the path we used that morning was covered with ice and rocks as big as cars—making us wonder if we could have outrun it or not.

Although Phil did mention the danger of avalanches more than a couple of times, the danger was obvious. When we reached the other side of the basin, I stepped into the next danger which was not so obvious when I experienced one thing always in the back of my mind: heart palpitations.

This was my Achilles heel, and it upset me. I no longer could climb in peace because my heart was hammering out a beat of 1-3, 1-5, 1-2, 1-6, a very irregular rhythm. My heart felt like a Mexican jumping bean, with a hard 'thump' every third beat.

I got mad and went silent, as though I could snub them to death. That might not be wise. There was nothing I could do about it. Usually, I would go to bed and sinus rhythm would return in my sleep to relieve me from the pounding irregularity. No chance of that here. I was thinking, God, please not now. I hadn't experienced heart palpitations while climbing in the mountains since Denali, nine years earlier.

What do you think I was going to do? Take a dime and call my mother? Yell to Phil to stop the bus, I'm getting off? I pondered other options before determining I didn't have any. I was going to suffer.

And to suffer meant more than feeling bad. Palpitations also decreases your heart's physical ability to perform efficiently by 35 percent; meaning, with my heart sputtering out of control, it only retained 65 percent of its natural ability to feed me oxygen for the climb.

The palpitations robbed me of 35 percent of my capacity to lift, hike, and pull myself up the mountain using little more than half strength. I decided not to tell Phil because I didn't want to explain the reason for my lack of strength. I wasn't looking for an excuse to explain anything. I'd be a person of lesser strength, a 'weakling' for lack of a better word, but a weakling who intended to make the summit.

But it didn't make me feel good to say so, because I didn't know if it was true.

We kept climbing below the ridge, working through the dawn hours as we came upon the Gun Barrels. This phenomenon lies atop an outcropping of boulders on the Shelf, high and away, towards the end of Linda Glacier. The Gun Barrels shoot real rocks at you like bullets dancing down the glacier—care to play Russian Roulette?

As the snow and ice softens during the day, these gun barrels release loose rocks down the same gulley you're climbing up. And those rocks come screaming by you as they shoot down the ice from the boulders. They seemingly come from nowhere and you sure don't want to get hit. Phil called it the "shooting gallery."

This was the real reason for starting the climb at 2:00 AM. If everything was frozen, you could make your way across the couloir with little chance of getting hit. A rock would blast from the gun barrels, say, once every two minutes. And it took a half-hour to get across the couloir (necessary because it connects the Linda Glacier with the Linda Shelf, and the NE Ridge to the summit). That's half an hour to cross the couloir, divided by a shot every two minutes, making it a dangerous fifteen shot crossing. Or a wild turkey shot at you 15 times as you're crossing the couloir. Phil went first.

Thus, the name "shooting gallery" is appropriate when trying to cross the target area without being shot. (It doesn't shoot anything, that's the effect.) But whatever those odds may be, it's a different story when descending off the Shelf in the afternoon. Then it's shooting a rock every thirty seconds.

MT. COOK

The bottom of the Shelf is where the granite meets the glacier. From that point forward it was straight up the granite wall for seven pitches, and you had to be roped in due to the extreme exposure. (Reminder: 1 rope length = 80 meters, 1 rope length = 1 pitch, Therefore, 1 pitch = 80-meter, 7 X 1 pitch = 560 meters, 1 meter converted to feet = 3.28 ft., 560 meters converted to feet = 1,836 ft.) Seven pitches is the equivalent of 1,836 feet. I know this because I just made the rest of the world adjust to American standards. Is that man enough for you?

I didn't know it would take that much climbing. The only other granite face I faced was the headwall on Denali, the one that broke the spirit of Ace and Jennifer so much so they went home. That 65 percent granite headwall was 1,000 feet, covered in ice and demanded we jumar up four pitches. This granite wall is much steeper and demanded we climb seven pitches, almost twice as high as Denali's headwall and two-thirds the size of El Capitan.

The beauty of climbing the Shelf of Mt. Cook, however, is there are handholds to be found. No searching around for a tiny crack to stand on, there'd be an actual ledge for your crampons. When you reach for a hand hold, there's a big nub of granite you can grab. And so on we climbed, moving over rock in tandem until we got to the end of the final pitch.

"Hey Phil," I said, still breathing hard from climbing. "I've been watching you. The way your body moves so easy, quick and graceful like, how do you do it?"

"Think about this Mark. Your body can move quickly and gracefully too, the secret is spending 320 nights a year outside in the mountains. You do that and you'll learn to move like a cat," said Phil.

I thought about that and how he had the edge on me there. Then I wondered if that was true. Could I move cat-like across this massive rock if I spent 320 nights consecutively outdoors?

"Nah," I said, "I'm sure it comes naturally, from DNA. Everything does, that's why you spend 320 nights out, right"

"Explain what?" Phil said.

"What you were talking about," I said.

"I was talking 320 nights." Phil said again.

"That's a long time...outdoors." (pause) (longer pause) "How much further?"

This is where the pep talk came in. The same one used in the Matterhorn Chapter as an example of inspiring pep talks, as opposed to being called a "fucking pussy."

MT. COOK

"Well, "Maaach," (his New Zealand enunciation) we're getting close. That last pitch was a bitch, wasn't it? I know I'm tired. But here's the deal, now it's going to get tougher, front pointing up this wall of ice isn't easy, but the summits right there, Mark. I bet you'd be disappointed if you got back to Santa Barbara and didn't finish this climb off?"

Who could take offense to that? "You're goddamn right Red Rider!"

But what I really said was, "Fuck, are you kidding me?

Before me was my nemesis. The photo of the climber with an ice axe in each hand, front pointing up the ice cap to the summit. That was the photo of the climber I wanted to be. But I'd never front pointed with two ice axes and had no idea how much concentration, strength, and stamina it took to pull it off, particularly above 12,000 feet. Front pointing up a 65% grade with both arms flying, axes stabbing the ice to keep steady, as you high step through the snow - it's a coordination nightmare, but a thing of beauty if done right.

"Here, you're going to need this," said Phil, handing me a hand ice axe.

"Oh, thanks," I said, staring at the smaller handheld ice axe. "For me?"

Phil looked at me and smiled, "Only until you get to the top, mate."

I made it to the top. It wasn't a thing of beauty.

Thing of Fantasy

I quit. The palpitations took over and kicked my ass. I was breathing hard…heart beating wildly…face drawn…short breaths. I couldn't hide the symptoms anymore.

I watched Phil take off like a snow leopard, jumping from crouch to crouch, up the ice, quick and graceful, to the summit. Then he looked down at me and yelled, "wooh, ooh." His way of saying, "Come on up."

I tried; I really did. But I started out like an old bear pulling himself up a hill. First you put your one arm out, and you shake it all about, you put your right arm in and shake that one again…it was hopeless. I saw there was a bench seat off to the side of the ice cap and motioned Phil to come join me, which he did.

"Ahh, this is a nice spot you got here. Let's sit down and give it a rest, eh? How you feeling? Beautiful enough for you, Mark? Just look at what you got here."

I looked at what I got, and how much I paid for it. It was a conundrum. What I got was nothing less than unique.

MT. COOK

I could see west, across the South Pacific Ocean. And to the east is the Talisman Sea. And in between is the land of spiraled white peaks and hidden green valleys, as many as you can count. And there wasn't a cloud in the sky. A sunny, 29 degrees. It was glorious.

And all it cost me was disappointment. My atrial fibrillation had slowed me considerably. To the point I quit, and that smells of *impotencia*. How much further?" I asked.

"You're there, mate. Congratulations."

"No, I'm asking how much further to the top."

"To the top? We're ten feet from it. It's right up there," said Phil, motioning with his arm and thumb, to someplace beyond the ice cap we were resting against, "Don't worry about it."

"I am worried about it. I came to climb Mt. Cook, not just say I climbed it." I said, hoping he understood.

He did. "I'm telling you, you climbed it," he said. "The top is ten feet away, mate. I'll show you. Let's eat something now, but I'll show you on our way down." Which I understood meant we were on our way down. I didn't object.

He then added, "It was a 5,500-foot vertical gain from base camp. If you climbed 5,490 feet of it, you're as good as there."

"Oh, that's not true. Did I go to the end of the trail, to the very top? Until I couldn't go no more?" I said, sort of chuckling. Giddy about being there.

"You're funny Mark, thinking something so stupid should interfere with your mountain climbing experience."

"Well, what if Ed Hillary decided to stop at the Hillary Step? How do you suppose that would have impacted the mountain climbing history of Everest?"

"Everest was the goal for Hillary, that's for sure, but you can't mix that with your goal of this family climb. Your daughter's still counting on you, no?"

Thank Allah for Phil thinking of Aurora because I had not.

"You're right. I should have been thinking."

"Don't worry about it."

~

It was fun to think of Sir Edmund Percival Hillary romping around the slopes of Mount Cook as a 30-year-old young man. But 'romping' doesn't explain what he was doing there, nor does 30-years-old describe a young man.

Hillary was a little-known beekeeper born in Auckland, New Zealand, and Mt. Cook was a mountain to be feared. That's why Hillary was solicited to aid Harry Ayres, the *greatest* of New Zealand's guides, on his expedition to

MT. COOK

Mount Cook. It had been summited before but never from the South Ridge. They reached the peak January 30, 1948, and the south ridge was renamed the Hillary Ridge, as a result. This approach to the summit is exactly opposite of the Linda Glacier which is on the North side of the mountain. Hillary's notoriety from the Mt. Cook expedition earned him a spot on John Hunt's 1953 British team to Mt. Everest.

    You can hear opportunity knocking, can't you? When the first two climbers turned back from the summit of Mt. Everest due to foul oxygen equipment, there was Ed Hillary and Tenzing Norgay waiting in the wings of the tent at the South Col. Two days later, the duo made history by becoming the first men to set foot on the highest summit in the world.

    Ed Hillary got his chance to struggle with destiny. He achieved the world's dream of somebody standing on top of the highest point on the planet, with not a single bit of earth left under him to make him taller. The moment he took the picture of Tenzing Norgay, Edmund Hillary ascended the dreams of humanity. For the rest of his life he was hailed as a hero, particularly mine.

    Why?

Because of his ability to endure pain for the purpose of achieving a goal which affords him nothing in return. The mere act of climbing a mountain is the epitome of a dog biting on a rock. ...sheer stupidity. But, nevertheless, here we are.

One Mountain Short

I don't expect I'll ever share that feeling of elitism, of being one who ascended to the top. I'll never be able to say, "I summited Mt. Everest." Missing that mark has left me wounded. I can say, "I summited the Matterhorn," which sounds silly in comparison to Mt Everest, but it isn't. It was a 'must have' goal in my life, and I got it. It means diligence, persistence, time, and money. That's what it means.

Add Mt. Blanc to the Matterhorn, and though it doesn't stack up against Mt. Everest, it desecrates Mt. Elbrus. It's the glamor of Europe against the lug nut of Asia. Summiting the Matterhorn/Mt. Blanc puts Elbrus so far back in the commie regime you can't see it. For the last time, get rid of Elbrus as a member of Seven Summits, and take Mount Jayawijaya with it.

For the Record

Our summit from Mt. Cook was picturesque. I got a panoramic shot of Phil on the South Pacific Ocean side of the range, and me, on the Talisman Sea side of the range. The mountain peaks were pinnacling through the glaciers spread below us. The chances of getting a view like that from the top of the ice cap was slim, maybe the same odds as getting hit with a rock shot from the Gun Barrels on the way down.

Knowing that, we plunged through the snow extra wide to get as far away as possible from the aim of the Gun Barrels. We had been toiling for ten hours, so Phil and I decided to sit down and eat lunch. I can't remember what we ate, but it was spread before us. I was sitting like I would in a chair, my legs bent at the knees, dangling my feet off the rock ledge we were sitting on.

We were in mid conversation when out of the blue, there comes from behind us the whine of a rock the size of my fist. It came flying, and I mean it came with a high-pitched whine whistling in my ears just moments before it smacked my left knee, striking me with such force, I yelled at the top of my lungs the following phrase:

"Motherfuckencocksuckensonofabitchafterbirthlickengonorea,piorea, syphilis, crabs, clap, shit that hurt!"

Phil, sitting a couple of feet away, didn't say a word. He observed me. I wasn't done by a long shot either. I grabbed that portion of my upper knee and began rubbing it profusely, violently even, an involuntary effort to make sure it wasn't broken into pieces. Rubbing it to see if there was life in it. It turned out the rock missed my knee and hit directly on the muscle above the kneecap.

My first impression was my leg got ripped off by a buzzing saw blade. By the time the pain subsided, I noticed the palpitations in my heart were gone. Just like that, my heart was ticking like a Timex, and steady as a rock. How lucky can one guy be? Free at last! I felt great.

Phil approached me cautiously. He sounded astute with his Kiwi accent, but he could just as well have been describing his ice axe when he said,

"You know Mark, the fact that rock set you off howlin' and screamin' like that, was actually a good sign. I was analyzing your symptoms, and yelling's a good one. It would have been bad if you weren't able to yell like that."

"Is that right?"

"Sure enough. If you hadn't of been yelling like that, I'd thought you were injured bad."

"You're saying if a guy yells and screams, he must be okay?"

"Yeah, that spontaneous yelling after sustaining injury, if I couldn't see you, I'd know you were okay. Says so in the manual."

"Says so in the manual, well, what's the alternative? Whimper or cry if you have a serious problem?"

"Moan, or just be dead," said Phil, giving me that matter-of-fact face.

"Thanks for the talk, Phil."

Impossible to Say

We were running out of time. When we sat to eat it was high noon, which gave us about an hour to get off the mountain. It was still clear and sunny, so we didn't feel rushed until we saw the cloud. A dark cloud rising over the plateau and coming straight for us. Those black clouds get uglier, bigger and angrier every time one crawls out from behind the horizon.

That's when Phil pulled out his Sat-phone and made the call for the helicopter.

"I didn't know you had Sat-phone on you."

"I only use it for emergencies."

"This is an emergency?" I asked.

"Look at that fucking cloud," he said, staring at the blackness, "That's the storm cloud and it looks like hell's coming with it. We'll be stuck in the Hut for a week."

"Let's get out of here."

My last recollection of Mount Cook aka Mt. Aoraki is seeing the black cloud engulf the sun. It descended over the snowy cliffs that befell the avalanches the day before. We ran the last 200 yards to the helicopter. Aurora grabbed her gear from the Hut and was running too. After racing through knee-deep snow, we met at the chopper and fled the scene. We wanted to get to the Lodge before it started to rain, and when it did rain it was turbulent. The black cloud was throwing steel-ball hail stones at us, and those things hurt.

We retreated to the Hermitage Hotel Lodge victorious, coming to rest in their lounge, just in time for dinner. As smelly and dirty as we were, Aurora, Phil, and I were hailed as heroes for conquering their precious highest mountain, and we had the appetites to prove it. The New Zealanders are at their best when being friendly.

This *is* the land that spawned the most celebrated mountain climber in history: Sir Edmund Hillary. He

MT. COOK

achieved what no man, or woman, had ever done. And it can't be done again. You're only first once.

The first question I'm *always* asked is, "Did you summit Everest?" My reply, "no" always reminds me of what I will never be able to say. People are always disappointed to hear I didn't summit Mt. Everest. There is no substitute for it. It's as though I'm not allowed to have a mountain climbing legacy without summitting Everest.

I can say, "I summited Mt. Denali in Alaska." I can assure you that means something to everybody. But I don't know what. To me it means I had the right temperament to climb that monster and came up a winner.

"I almost summited Mt. Aconcagua in Argentina." I was stopped 400 feet from the top, which was a dirty shame. But look at all the blessings it gave me: My harmonic convergence with Tom Taplin; my friend, Mike Larrabee, a two-time gold medal winner, who died at age 69, and Valentin Trenev, who was my guide for a decade.

"I summited Kilimanjaro." That summit is a duo; it brought me my beautiful wife D'Arcy, whom I couldn't live without.

"I summited Mt. Cook." Did I? I did and came away with the memory of the last Christmas vacation I shared with my daughter.

"I summited the Matterhorn/Mount Blanc in place of Elbrus. Who blames me? Mount Blanc still is the highest mountain in Europe.

That leaves me with one mountain more on the list of seven continental summits to climb: Vinson Massif, Antarctica.

Veni, Vide, Vici. I came, I saw, I conquered. Or not.

Phil Penny, guide extraordinaire!

Father and daughter in New Zealand

Aurora Maxine Cornwall with her proud dad

MT. KILIMANJARO, TANZANIA (2000)

18.

A Plane to Nairobi

Any questions I had about D'Arcy, I expected to get answered on Kilimanjaro.

What better place to learn about a future lover than climbing the highest mountain in Africa? I couldn't wait to watch her barter for toilet paper and beer with the locals. D'Arcy was having her thirtieth birthday on the very day we climbed aboard KLM flight 849 to Amsterdam. Next stop, Nairobi. As we were waiting in the lobby to leave on the first leg of the trip to Amsterdam, I decided to make one last appeal for an upgrade since it was D'Arcy's birthday.

A fifty-year-old attorney, traveling with his thirty-year-old lover, on whose birthday he is taking her to Africa to climb the highest mountain on the continent, can make a real sweet argument when asking for another seat assignment. I tugged on every heart string available to make this moment romantic.

It was a chance of a lifetime for D'Arcy (with no stamps in her passport indicating she had never gone anywhere) to get special recognition because she was traveling to Kilimanjaro on her actual birthday. "Look at her license. It says August 30, 1970. That's today! Her birthday is today."

That steward was the first of several to ask if I intended to propose on the summit of Kilimanjaro. One attendant later assured me her brother proposed to his fiancée on the summit, and he was gay! (What's that supposed to mean?) "Yes, of course, just give us an upgrade." But the purser made no promises, and we moved on down the line.

As we approached the entry to the plane where passengers were crowding around the portal, we saw the same ticket person watching as each passenger was motioned to their seat assignments. It was always, "to the right," the purser would say, "to the right." When it was our turn, the purser stepped forward to D'Arcy and said, "This way for you," and took us to the left. There, before our eyes, was the most voluminous overnight cabin the sky has to offer, commonly referred to as First Class.

As if the full-length sleepers were not enough, she positioned us in front so we could have the private suite. Without a doubt, this flight was the only way to travel to Amsterdam from L.A. When the flight attendant presented us with the complimentary alabaster blue and white bottles of alcohol in the shape of Ann Frank's house, we nearly peed our pants.

Our luck stopped there at Amsterdam Schiphol Airport. We switched commercial liners for the six-hour flight from Amsterdam to Nairobi, to Nairobi Airways. The crew told us over the loudspeaker there would be no in-flight movie because an employee took the movie cassette home with him. *We had no movie on a six-hour flight because an employee stole the movie.* That movie was to be *Big Mama's House.* Although we found that comical, because we were flying to Africa, we could have used the Tyler Perry special for diversion on the flight. Well, welcome to Nairobi anyway!

No Way to Treat a Lady?

I've never heard Mt. Kilimanjaro referred to as sexy, but my vision of the highest mountain in Africa is palpable sensuality. The image of Venus di Milo comes to mind, the goddess of love, lying lasciviously across the Serengeti plains. Her full hips touch the sky with white cream melting down her crevasse. Provocative indeed! Kilimanjaro projects a statuesque figure of both virility and fertility with loins a-blazing. Nothing could better represent the world's equatorial mid-section than a thatched roof above a smoldering crater. I fell in love with Kilimanjaro, as I was falling in love on Kilimanjaro.

The personality of Mt. Kilimanjaro as a woman is the same as the five temperate zones you walk through on the way to her summit. The five-day trek to the summit begins in the 5,000-foot comfort zone of coffee and lush vegetation. You pass through a rainforest of monkeys, filled with green moss and yellow songbirds. Wearing your light rain jacket to protect against the heavy mist of the forest, you rip it off at 9,000 feet, as you step out of the mist, and into the arid Alpine Desert. You'll be greeted by groves of green succulents spotting the vast expanses of space.

Above that, it's all rocky brown volcanic dirt. The birds have turned into the same big black crows you hear squawking all over the world above 10,000 feet. Only these have a white widget under each wing. It is the only place on earth where you can go from damp jungle to arid desert within ten feet. That's pretty darn unique.

My new "girlfriend" and I marveled at these strange eco conditions as we walked at the tail end of our thirteen-member expedition. Our group was made up of old climbing buddies, their friends, and wives. It was the sixth of my *Seven Summits* climbs, and the first attempt at climbing any mountain by my companion, D'Arcy.

MT. KILIMANJARO

I purposely saved this mountain for when I was fifty years old. That was the plan, and I was sticking to it. The reason for waiting was that I needed every ounce of youth and vigor to challenge the more difficult climbs earlier in life.

The conditions on Everest, Denali, Aconcagua and even Mt. Cook show no mercy. The dead are often left behind to save the lives of those remaining. They can be retrieved next season. When that angry black cloud appears unexpectedly and it's screaming "I'm going to freeze you to death;" it can sound scary.

You're never going to see that black cloud while climbing Kilimanjaro, but rumors of Kilimanjaro being a "walk in the park" are dangerous. It's the only mountain I ever climbed where, much to the dismay of my young climbing partner, two people were carted off the mountain on gurneys, dressed in orange body bags. In both cases their hearts just quit.

This made my girlfriend wonder if I had taken out a life insurance policy on her. Not a very romantic thought. But the fact is, the rim of this crater is 19,341 feet high, and comes with all the attenuating altitude hazards. For example, there is only half the oxygen on top of the crater as there is at the bottom.

D'Arcy spent her years before climbing Kilimanjaro very differently from mine. She was an avid skier growing up in Reno, but the mountains were not a regular part of her life. She did have one great physical advantage over me, however: she was twenty years younger. There is no substitute for youth.

She competed on her high school women's basketball team as point guard and led them not only to the league championship, but to the Nevada State Championship. They won, and she was honored as the tournament's MVP. I was impressed. It gave me insight into her competitive nature which was not apparent from talking to her. She was also a "star golfer" when I met her, who unwittingly taught lessons to male golfers that worried about losing to a woman. I was proud of her for that.

D'Arcy came to work in our office as a legal secretary about two years before climbing Kilimanjaro. I paid no attention to her because legal secretaries come and go. I had enough problems with my own secretary. I had just fired mine for embezzlement. From purchasing office furniture to forging checks from the trust. That not only made me mad, it hurt me.

MT. KILIMANJARO

D'Arcy was going to law school at the time with one of the other secretaries from my office. I met her one night, when they were studying in the office library. Since I was the owner of the building, I decided to give them shit about the cost of electricity and who was going to pay for it.

But the real reason I gave them shit was because I'd gotten thunderstruck by D'Arcy. She was wearing a black turtleneck, with her blond hair pulled back in a ponytail, so her bangs framed her face; it made her features look strikingly sophisticated for a young woman. Her dangling earrings made her look sexy rather than cute. Being single, I paused for a moment. But that was just a glance, besides- she was married.

She was still married when she came to work in my office, but law school has a way of spoiling marital bliss. As they say, the first divorce you handle after law school will be your own. That proved true for me, and who needs any part of someone else's divorce? About a year prior to departing for Kilimanjaro, office reshuffling put D'Arcy to work reporting to me.

This is when things got interesting. I began having fun practicing law again. I love sports, and D'Arcy's knowledge of the game, any game, demanded she be taken seriously. Her ability to identify professional athletes and understand how they play the game allowed her to talk football with the best of them. That was new. With that mindset comes the associated sense of humor shared universally by all sports lovers, whether it's commentators or locker room jocks.

I had a girlfriend at the time who was more the runway model style, but she hated sports. That ruled out everything I've written above concerning humor. A friend once saw her walking down the street and told me she "exuded sex". That may be great in the bedroom, but while walking down the street? She bragged about being a member of MENSA too, whatever that is. And if being a know-it-all wasn't bad enough, she was an attorney to boot.

But worse than that, and I mean I should have run when she told me this: She hated her father. So, when D'Arcy told me she was going to run a marathon in Lake Tahoe in the Spring just for fun, and do it with her brother, I thought she was God's gift to normalcy.

Between the office managing embezzler, and the father-hating sex addict, I began to wonder, when it came to women, if I had become blind to women who would betray me. My level of trust hit an all-time low. But I'm no misogynist. I love women, and I sure as hell ain't no cynic.

MT. KILIMANJARO

In the months before Kilimanjaro, our relationship grew from a puritan ethic into a platonic friendship. Since the law did not allow a sexual nexus in the workplace, we stuck to our motto, "Perfection is our standard, not our goal," as we worked side by side. We did that until I finally asked her for our first date. And that was after she separated from her husband.

I admit to being stuck in a predicament concerning our job relationships. It was a sticky situation, a boss and secretary going to climb Kilimanjaro. But my solution to this problem seemed reasonable at the time. The question to D'Arcy was simple. And I don't recall making more of it at the time than, say, asking her to assist me at a deposition in San Francisco for a couple of days. All business, but still fun.

I decided to give her the option of choosing between being laid off for the month of August, or… "You could come with me to climb Kilimanjaro. We'll go on safari after the climb, perhaps explore the Seychelles Islands, then head back to Europe and hit Amsterdam, and then we'll drive to Octoberfest in Bavaria on our way home—all on me. What do you say, D'Arcy?"

The biggest part of that question is what does it take to climb Kilimanjaro?

That question is normally answered by genetics, subject to change on any climb. If you have never climbed at altitude, you have no idea how your body will acclimate due to lack of oxygen. Some bodies refuse to work if they ascend the mountain too rapidly. This causes high-altitude pulmonary edema (HAPE), which can kill you within hours if not brought to a lower elevation immediately. You'll recognize the symptoms too late if your motor nerves shut down and you can't get your gloves on or off.

Another common quirk of altitude's effect on one's body is refusing to eat. We took five days for the climb to have time for acclimatization. Our party stopped for an extra rest day at Horombo Hut at 12,120 feet, just to lake certain we had a chance to acclimatize. D'Arcy was eating double helpings of tomatoes and cucumbers, both there and at the Kibo Hut 15,420 feet, the last hut before the summit. She exhibited no symptoms of altitude sickness.

I, on the other hand, had no appetite by the time we got to Kibo. But I had enough experience to monitor my strength to the summit. I knew I could make it if I drank plenty of fluids. You can always buy a liter of beer from an ambitious porter on Kilimanjaro.

~

Why Mountain Climbing?

In every book about mountain climbing, whether to the Seven Summits or elsewhere, the author asks why people climb. And my answer is, after, "The desire to test your mettle against nature's powerful swift sword," comes, "We climb to share the camaraderie of new friends, fighting the odds against making the summit, pushing our bodies and minds to find the extreme, and then pushing beyond it," wrote my friend, Tom Taplin, who died on Everest in 2015 in his sleep.

As Tom Taplin wrote in his book *The Stone Sentinel*, "Climbing represents a dream in which both the longing for adventure and the hardships endured has the opportunity to be balanced by a newfound camaraderie and the discovery of previously untapped reserves of will-power."

I love the dream of camaraderie that goes with mountaineering. It puts you and every climber that stands before the mountain to the test. There is no guarantee those relationships forged under the rigors of the climb are going to last. Even when you shared the biggest victory of your life with your new best friend, that relationship rarely finds its way off the mountain. The energy created on the path of adventure cannot be duplicated. It fades and becomes a memory, and after years, the memory becomes fog and is forgotten.

MT. KILIMANJARO, TANZANIA (2000)

19.
Wives and Girlfriends

There are several reasons for inviting wives and girlfriends on this climb to the iconic Kilimanjaro. The roundness of the crater for one. Its popularity, from a view standpoint, is different from the other Seven Summits. It stands alone, literally, erupting from the Serengeti plains, casting its 25-mile-wide volcanic shadow across the darkest of the seven continents. Its 16,000-foot vertical height from base to rim, makes it the highest free-standing mountain in the world—and we took five days to get to the summit and back.

Kilimanjaro is as identifiable by the snow around its crater, as the Matterhorn, another free-standing mountain, is identifiable by the shape of its granite horn protruding from the European Alps. The Matterhorn's face was chiseled by receding glaciers, honed to a pinnacle reaching for heaven, while Mt. Kilimanjaro's lava explodes from her crater, creating the cradle of civilization, covered with obsidian ash. You can feel the sexual tension being exploited. It's Mark and D'Arcy's.

The best "creature comforts" Kilimanjaro offers are the porters. They help climbers to enjoy the scenery, rather than struggle with their bags. That is huge! What a joy to frolic about the landscape unburdened by your expedition pack. That's not just a choice you get to make either, it's the law. There are unemployed men in Tanzania who depend on carrying your gear to make a living, and the rules of the Tanzania National Park system assure the tourists provide them with this work.

You pay for it in terms of the permit. You may not want a porter, but you pay for one anyway. They are all good guys that can help you in many ways. They can get you cold beers. And equally important is their connection to toilet paper which gets very sparse the higher you go. They work on a barter system that can get you hot water in the morning, extra food, dry gear, batteries, or any other necessity, in exchange for money.

As for the climb, they care for you in every detail. Whatever their size or look (and they look ragged) they are all very strong, and good natured on the trail. You don't have to ask for assistance either. They are not like the Argentinian guides—the porters on Kilimanjaro are there to carry your burden, not make it a burden. Their oppositeness to Americans allows them to be free in the culture of their continent and feel good about it. Yes, of course, it would be nice if you tipped them. That's what makes the world go around. For very little in return, you get a lifetime of memories.

On our summit day, Mr. Larrabee had a sudden attack of vertigo while climbing the mountain. He was discovered by porters who stepped in to help immediately. Mike caught vertigo not long after we started the climb from Kibo Hut. The motion of climbing one foot forward, two steps back, made him dizzy as he tried to navigate the scree switchbacks. Two porters carried him back, one under each arm because he had no balance. For that he tipped them $50.00.

No Summit for You

The other person that suffered an attack on summit day was another experienced climber. I climbed Mont Blanc with her the summer before with her as my tent mate. Although a strong climber on Mont Blanc, she failed to make the cut on Kilimanjaro. She should have turned back the same as Mike, after her unforgiveable act of throwing up on everybody in Hans Meyer's Cave.

Maybe if she hadn't been so experienced, or if she was young and stupid, it could be explained. I would feel some compassion. But you can't tell me she didn't feel that vomit coming up from her stomach while she was still outside the cave. And if she could have chosen to throw up outside the cave, that'd be one thing...but nooooooo! She ran in and barfed all over us.

The cave, named after the first summiteer of Kilimanjaro in 1889, is used as a much-needed resting spot for all climbers, and it was crowded on the morning of our climb. It provides relief from the outside elements. If ever there was a moment in climbing history, for this climber to excuse herself from the climb, it was right then. But instead, it was her response to allow a porter to assist her from the cave, by pulling her by the hand, step by step, for the last 500 feet, to reach the summit at Gillman's Peak—as though she was a princess.

From her standpoint, she used the porter to cheat the mountain out of its summit. That's what a porter can also do for you. If anybody believes her behavior is somehow heroic, or proves she is no quitter, or is a display of true grit, or that this was practical or reasonable behavior under the circumstances, you don't understand the sport of mountaineering. It was a demeaning act, an affront to everyone that had to watch. The hero would have controlled their pains of inner conflict, not barfing on her fellow climbers. Oh well.

Perhaps my response to her conduct came from her unapologetic behavior after the fact. Her recollection of events deleted her need for help. In fact, she ridiculed other climbers who summited Uhuru Peak for using Diamox, a medication which creates more red blood cells to carry more oxygen, rumored to help climbers at high altitude.

I have never used Diamox, but this climber could only wonder aloud, very loudly in a crowded room, whether she had taken the drug, "like the others," perhaps she would not have felt so sick when reaching Hans Meyer's Cave.

That was the measure of her thinking.

The second reason for choosing Kilimanjaro as a romantic getaway is purely pragmatic. Because it is a "non-technical" climb, you have no need for mountaineering experience. There's no other mountain in the world over 19,000 feet where fundamental knowledge of cold weather gear, boots and crampons, climbing on ice, ice axe usage, ropes and crevasse training, and frostbite awareness do not come in handy. D'Arcy had no background in any of these unique skills, and she was no less prepared.

Other than wondering if she had signed her life away on any last-minute papers before we left home, D'Arcy approached mountain climbing with as positive an attitude as the rigors in altitude will allow. There is significant hardship on a mountain the size of Kilimanjaro that gets lost in any written account of the climb. The translation between living the action and putting it into words always fails to tell the true story. So, this is as true as it gets.

Kilimanjaro is blessed with a series of huts to help take the grind out of roughing it with tents. Although, these huts leave something to be desired. The normally travelled route begins at the Marangu Gate, at an elevation of 5,880 feet. The first night is spent Mandara Hut, at 9,000 feet. The second night is at Horombo Hut at 12,334 feet. The third night you attempt to sleep until 11:00 p.m. at Kibo Hut, 16,250 feet. The plan is: You get up and start the climb at midnight. You climb to the summit, watch the sun rise, then head all the way back to Horombo Hut for the night. The next night you are hopefully enjoying a festive party at the Kibo Hotel in Marangu.

The trek along this *normal* route is five days and four nights at the huts. Our group spent an extra night at Horombo Hut to give everyone an extra day as stated. The only way to feel comfortable above the 12,334-foot elevation is to give your body time to acclimate. The team effort on these expeditions is to give encouragement to those climbers who feel nauseous or otherwise weak from altitude sickness.

D'Arcy's the Bomb

Those conditions never described D'Arcy's state of physical being. The two days we kicked back at Horombo Hut she maintained the nature of a girl away at summer camp. The camp itself was made up of one big A-frame for gathering and eating, and a dozen other A-frame cottages with four to ten single bunk beds in each. They call them Alpine Huts, presumably because the camp is located on the open expanse of the Shira Plateau called the Alpine Desert.

The problem is there is nothing to see in the surrounding area which qualifies as a typical Alpine scene. It's not Alpine, it's prehistoric. The earth looks like millions of years of packed volcanic gravel which bears no semblance to the green recesses between granite peaks in the European Alps.

The peak of Kilimanjaro is an oval-barren expanse. There are no competing summits to add to the beauty. What it does have that gets closer with every step, is its pure massiveness. Unique in its stature, it stands alone, defiantly, as if to say, "I don't need no fucking peak. I am the mother of all peaks. This is my continent. Deal with it."

Against this backdrop, the A-frame huts look somewhat out of place. This was not D'Arcy's point of view, however. She ran around the mess hall like a social director, engaging everybody she met from any country, or with any political agenda or disposition, and had a story to tell.

If I chose to lay in a field and watch clouds dance between my fingers, she would come back excited about the arrival of the Spanish Climbing Team all dressed sharply alike, or the Belgian guitar player serenading Katherine, or the latest news on the medic running the British emergency team. She got us a steaming bowl of hot water in the morning and our own roll of toilet paper from the porters. What a gal!

While everybody's appetite began to wane, she surprisingly ate more of the corn porridge and avocado, tomato, and cucumber sandwiches that were available. She was happy to hike up the trail for a couple of miles of extra elevation to help acclimatize. Do you have any idea how hard that is to find in a partner? In someone you love? What I'm saying is, she did not complain!

MT. KILIMANJARO

Those are great attributes for any person in your life, but we're talking about a beautiful young woman. I used to marvel at the lack of beautiful women in the mountains. It's not hard to find a choir to preach to on the subject, particularly high up, around the campfire. It makes good sense because climbing, hiking, trekking, just walking on a mountain trail, is dangerous.

I was hiking a very neat trail up to Vernal Falls in Yosemite one time, stepped wrong on a rock under my tennis shoes, and broke the metatarsal in my right foot. It's an injury common amongst ballet dancers, and one that could happen to anybody on a simple hike. I ended up with a boot on for six weeks. Why would a beautiful woman risk breaking her foot while taking a hike, when she could meet all the gentlemen she desired at home? As superficial as that sounds, it is true. Girls don't go camping alone.

D'Arcy was not that type of girl. From the very first step through Marangu Gate, in Tanzania National Park, in the presence of twelve other climbing mates walking together, we were all alone. We were two lovebirds oblivious to the rest of the world. We always let the others go ahead of us, as we walked behind, falling further in love. We were always the very last ones in the procession. If they slowed down, we went slower. We wanted the tail end so we could be as far away as possible, *non-interruptus*.

We finally got our chance at the Horombo Huts. We shared a four-bunk hut with John Bragg and his wife. John was the absolute best life-long friend of Mike Larrabee. They climbed Aconcagua together at age 55, the same time as me in 1989. In fact, that's where we met, on the switchbacks up to *Nido*.

Warm by mountain standards at 13,000 feet, it was cool enough to feel cozy, snuggled together in our bags, head to head. Our bunks were on the floor, perpendicular along the two walls, joined in the corner of the hut. Making love comes in so many fascinating ways it's difficult to explain exactly how it happened. But in that moment, D'Arcy was in her most vulnerable form, as was I, hanging in there with me, 13,000 feet up Mt. Kilimanjaro.

We were finally alone, completely naked in our thoughts, where we could only see ourselves together. We had no pretensions, no more laughing, or joking, as we made our way in spirit to the top of Africa. Our minds met upon life's essentials, embraced each other's heart and soul, loved what we saw, and refused to let go of it.

No, I won't reveal the particulars of that scene, going frame by frame through our love. The physical challenge for us laid ahead. Kilimanjaro looked like the shape of a brown raison laying on the plain. It became more apparent with every step toward the summit. The closer we got, the more we realized how each nook and cranny of the volcanic mass was part of a giant gilded wall that made up the 25-mile circumference of the crater that was two miles wide.

As the shadows of cracked and faulted magma grew more immense, a trail emerged from the residue of exploded lava called "scree." The scree is an accumulation of vented hot-rock-debris, layering the face of the volcanic slopes with black gravel. There is no bottom to it, much the same as quicksand—two steps up, one-foot slides back, seemingly forever, or until you get to the top.

Add to this, the higher we go the less air there is to breathe. Climbing at altitude is the science of atmospheric pressure. There is exactly half the air pressure at 19,000 feet as there is at sea level. That means when your boot keeps getting stuck in a pile of stone rubble causing you to yank it out and place it a step higher in the heap, before it gets sucked down again, you have exactly half the volume of air to breathe while performing the same task at sea level. The hyperventilating necessary (the repetitive breathing in and out, deep and fast, to catch your breath) can get tiresome after a couple of hours. For many, it becomes exhaustion too much to bear.

The distance between Horombo Hut and Kibo Hut, the last hut at 16,000 feet, is six miles. You gain 3,000 feet in altitude but lose 10 percent more oxygen. During those six miles, you pass the elevation of 14, 505 feet. You know you're with the right people when one of them, in this case, Mike Larrabee, stops his fellow climbers to make an announcement.

There were thirteen of us in the group. Mike picked out nine for a photograph. I did not have the slightest idea why. Checking the altimeter on his watch he informed us we had just passed the elevation of Mt. Whitney, California. These nine mountain-climbing novices had just climbed higher than the highest mountain on the continental United States.

It was a thoughtful thing to do. I wish I had thought of it for D'Arcy. It gave the four climbers who chose not to attempt the summit time to reflect on what they achieved, rather than what they chose to avoid on the mountain. Funny, this act of kindness coming from a two-time Olympic Gold Medal winner who thinks second place is for the first loser. Now these four women climbers would have a photo of them trekking higher than anybody on the Continental United States. Celebrate your victories.

For the rest of us, our journey to Kibo was rewarded by long lines of uneasy climbers waiting their chance to use the shitters behind the hut. There are two green doors that separate the latrines outside, dug too shallow a long time ago, from the anxious defecators suffering from a plague of intestinal diseases. These climbers couldn't hit a 12" hole in the floor with their own turds. If the goal of this filthy fiasco was to set a record for repulsive filth, they got it.

There are no records of how many climbers attempted to shit in these holes, but by my count most of them missed. After one trip to the latrines D'Arcy and I decided to take our business elsewhere, no matter how far we had to walk—only to find somebody had already been there.

MT. KILIMANJARO, TANZANIA (2000)

20.

The Endless Summit

You have six hours to relax at the Kibo Hut before you must leave for the summit at midnight. That was plenty of time for D'Arcy to enjoy her favorite dinner of tomatoes and cucumbers. And for me to give her a half-hour dissertation on the most efficient layering techniques for cold weather gear; designed for D'Arcy to carry the lightest load possible.

I started with the three pairs of long johns, then mitten liners, gloves, socks, boots, ankle guards, wind guards, baklavas, wool beanies, rain and wind jackets, belts, goggles, ski mask, when and where to use them, how to use them, where to pack them, adjusting the headlamp, what not to do while using them, staving off the first symptoms of frostbite, and how to keep hydrated. All things that keep you safe and comfortable.

As I was talking to her, the bunkhouse full of climbers preparing to challenge Kilimanjaro in the next hour fell silent. Even the biggest "know it all" of them all, Duane, shut his mouth to make a mental check of the tips I offered D'Arcy. Everybody had some performance anxiety about what they would face when they went outside the door to face it.

Everyone shared the same dream of coming to this exotic land for the purpose of being in this precise moment—readying to conquer Africa's highest mountain. The why of it was not the question. The fear of the mountain was what niggled them in the back of their minds. How to get it done is what they wanted to be sure of. Any little tip might help.

It was freezing black outside, well below zero. Headlamps were necessary. With the monolithic blackness in front of us, you could see a few white dots shining from twist and turns of the trail. What is different about summit day on Kilimanjaro is starting at midnight. The coldest part of night is still coming. And it's too early to have gotten any rest with twenty people coughing and hacking.

D'Arcy and I got the biggest surprise in the whole group. After trailing behind the rest of the gang for the last three days, our guide, Disario, decided it would be wise to put D'Arcy at the very front of our eight-member team, and keep me at the very back to bring up the rear. For the first time on our trip, we would be separated. What do I do?

It was a smart choice on Disario's part. He knew D'Arcy was an inexperienced climber but never had the opportunity to gauge her physical stamina, nor her desire to reach the top. All he saw was her loving on me. We were two lovers on the trail and D'Arcy was always last in a line of 13 people.

Naturally, Disario assumed D'Arcy was the slowest. Putting her directly behind him in the lead, served two purposes. Using her as the group's altimeter he could monitor her strength as we ascended the trail. This way Disario could determine the median pace for everyone. He couldn't do this with D'Arcy in the back.

The general rule for determining how fast a group of climbers will move is: The guide goes no faster than the slowest member of the team, as long as they get to the top before dawn. As Disario saw it, D'Arcy and I were the slowest coming up the mountain, so it made sense to have her first in line. It also assured the group the two of us wouldn't mess around, which pissed me off, but wasn't the time to talk about it.

His mistake was not talking to us before. When it came to serious business, that's what D'Arcy and I were all about. That's what we did for a living. Disario chose the wrong person to anticipate being slow on summit day.

MT. KILIMANJARO

From the start, every step Disario took D'Arcy was right behind him. I mean, it was as though D'Arcy was going to step into Disario's shoes. And as the climb progressed it looked funny to me. She became his shadow. Like Gumbo.

D'Arcy took his instructions to follow right behind him to mean, "put your foot in my boot print as soon as I lift up." Right, left, right, left. Quite literally, D'Arcy kept his pace, stepping onto his boot print as though she was riding the back draft from his body, like the wind spun off him to pull her forward. It looked like D'Arcy was chasing Disario!

Only it wasn't walking, it was climbing, and it was being done at 19,000 feet. That's no easy task. As the two became visible in the dawn hours, I could see Disario far ahead of the pack with D'Arcy right on his ass. The two of them were about twenty feet in front of the others. Where were they going? Disario would continuously stop to wait for the rest of us, and there would be D'Arcy, fit as a fiddle, waving at me.

The experienced climber, who will remain unnamed, would never admit it, but the pace is what took her down. She couldn't take it. Her body could not assimilate to the lack of oxygen, so she became nauseous, then her mind joined her sickness when she made the bad decision to throw up in the cave. It was the pace that did it.

D'Arcy was the first person to step on the summit at Gillman's Point, about one second after Disario. I was doing my duty at the rear with the porters where I learned that singing tribal chants helped ease the burden of pain. While others gasped for air and fought against frostbite in the freezing cold, I discovered the birth of the blues. The melody stepped in to replace the pain with joy. It was like a drug, and I liked it.

Struggling to Summit

Within the last 250 feet of the summit the line of climbers gets strewn apart as the pace disintegrates into personal breaks. A struggling climber must step aside for you to make a comfortable pass on the trail. I passed Katherine, Duane and John Bragg, so I could catch up to D'Arcy. When I finally reached the top of the rim of the crater, we went to kiss but our lips wouldn't pucker because our cheeks didn't stretch from the cold; we laughed and then I kissed her.

D'Arcy later told me her "fit as a fiddle" appearance while climbing may have been a bit deceiving. She never felt safe the whole way up, she said. She did not feel out of danger until the sun came up to show her more of the surrounding area. Regardless of her *fit as a fiddle* appearance, her fear of what was beyond her headlight motivated her more than the physical challenge of the mountain.

The entire six hour climb from Kibo had been done in the pitch black of night. D'Arcy's reality of the trail was restricted to the scope of her headlamp. She had no idea what was outside the scope of that torch. As far as she knew, once we got passed the monotonous scree climb, the rock path through the boulders may have led past 1,000-foot drop offs. How was she to know?

Her focus was on the boot print under Disario's boots. She was concentrating on each of his steps and hell-bent to place her foot exactly where Disario placed his. Nothing less would do. She did not want to be left in the dark. D'Arcy only felt safe if she walked in his exact steps.

Besides that, the altitude doesn't allow you to think more than one step ahead. An hour goes by. After that you can only think about stopping to rest. Goddamn, are we ever going to stop? Let's sing a chant. The ends of my fingers are numb. They're more numb than ever, they're freezing, what should I do?

"Mark," a 65-year-old climber, Gene Rasmussen, a retired judge, yells to me from up above, "My fingers are freezing! No feeling. What can I do?"

If a climber's circulation is not working to the tips of his fingers, despite the glove preventions taken, the fear of frostbite is real. It can ruin the trip. Something must be done, but no one wants to fall behind with a stop. I yelled back, "Pound your fingers on a rock, with your gloves on. Smack 'em on a rock, as hard as you can, a few times, until you feel the pain. That should do it." It must have worked— he thanked me later for the help.

~

The idea behind leaving at midnight is to give you time to watch the sunrise from the top Africa. Because you're only three degrees south of the equator you get the best of both the northern and southern hemispheres. The sun still rises in the east, (ha, ha) and from Gilman's Point you can look directly into the rising sun to see the second highest mountain in Africa, Mt. Kenya, about 2,000 feet lower in the foreground, 223 miles away as the crow flies.

The expanse of earth seen from the mountain top depends on the weather. It was crystal clear for us—you could see the ends of the earth. Not the horizon, but the arc

MT. KILIMANJARO

of the elliptical planet called Earth. You could only see the curvature because on this morning it was so bitter cold.

But what Kilimanjaro offers due to its temperate equatorial climate, is a chance to view the African Continent under more moderate conditions than any other continental summits. You don't have to fear an abrupt weather change that could kill you. That physical safety allows free play on the summit—particularly because of all the room on top of the crater. This made it so much more romantic to fall in love.

What you read into any sunrise depends on how you feel that morning. How did it feel for us to succeed in our adventure, sitting next to each other in the crescent of this most foreign land? Things could have ended so differently, like the two bodies we saw in orange body bags . It only takes a moment for dreams to turn to nightmares. But no! This was our love story, our panache of romance. I couldn't have dreamt a better highlight of my life at fifty, and now I have D'Arcy with me to live the rest of my life.

It was before twilight when we arrived at Gillman's Point. The dawn was obsidian; the horizon blended into the purple black sky. The sliver of moonlight we did have was of no use to us, and the sunrise did not start until 6:30.

The light from our headlamps reflected the porters' faces. These are Africans, not African Americans. Their friendly smiles exhaled frozen breath in the light of our headlamps. Again, it was cold. They were happy to take D'Arcy and my photo leaning on the brown and gold sign that read, Gillman's Point, 18,640 feet. Hoo-rah!

Disputed Summits

Our priority was getting those photos taken. As with most things surrounding D'Arcy and my life at that time, the photo taking was complicated. We needed one of us kissing behind the sign with all the love, but we also needed one with a porter or two between us for the business folks back home. We were not supposed to be lovers to the rest of the world; we were a business team. There was a standard of propriety to be met for our adversaries back at the courthouse.

There are several conditions making this photo difficult, besides the fact we were in the death zone at 19,000 feet. There is the exhaustion from a six-and-a-half-hour climb, the danger of standing around in the cold, the rush to get your photo taken before moving on to Uhuru Peak, or going back down, the confusion of everybody doing the same thing at once, and my pet peeve —having to

MT. KILIMANJARO

take three pairs of gloves and liners off to fumble with a camera, and risk frostbite.

The exhilaration you feel from the victory of success is offset by the same number of climbers who become nauseous, injured, or rendered totally numb by the event. For everyone, the hour long wait for the sun to rise was frustrated by the decision of what to do next. There was only one thing D'Arcy, and I wanted to do.

What we didn't want to do was spend the next four hours sucking for air as we walked around the crater to gain 500 feet so we could say, "Not only did we summit this monster volcano and enjoy ourselves, but we spent the next four hours dragging our ass over to Uhuru Peak and back, just for another picture."

But more than that, we didn't feel like spending any time on the tippy top of Kilimanjaro with the fellow climbers that were headed that way. That included Katherine and Duane, two very unhappy campers who were going to Uhuru Peak if it killed them.
John Bragg, our leader, who organized and led the trip, was so sick, his swollen face was turning bright pink to orange from fever. He stared vacantly as he explained his condition to me, then turned determinedly to follow the others to Uhuru. D'Arcy and I fell in behind John for about 100 yards

before I yelled to him, "We're going back to Gillman's to enjoy the sunrise!"

"Then you're going the wrong way," he yelled back painfully blunt.

The decision not to finish the climb to Uhuru was not taken lightly. I strongly believe in touching the very highest point on the mountain, not just standing near it. But the need to take that extra step just to make a point, faded into the question of why it was so important. Why is it so important to touch the highest point on the crater? "The circumstances surrounding this climb put the summit day focus in a different mood," is the only way I can answer that.

D'Arcy and I had other interests than Uhuru. I wanted to make love on top of the *Snows of Kilimanjaro*. One-up old Hemingway, so to speak. I wanted to bask in the golden rays of morn. I came for love, not trudging to Uhuru to make my heart go thunk.

The problem with that idea was the temperature. D'Arcy and I snuggled at Gillman's Point while watching the sun rise from our rock bed. It didn't take long to realize hugging and kissing in our heavy cold weather gear was not one of its recommended usages. And not stimulating enough to warm us against the cold.

MT. KILIMANJARO

Getting naked was out of the question. After a half hour our tongues stopped working because there was a fist of ice squeezing our larynx. That was enough. We headed back down. We were kicking up rooster tails in the scree, all the way to Kibo Hut like a couple of kids coming home from after-school playground.

Gene Rasmussen, the retired Municipal Court Judge from Lake Tahoe and three other 65-year-old buddies, including John and Duane, plus Katherine, went ahead and summited at Uhuru Peak. Everyone who summits Kilimanjaro, whether Gillman's Point or Uhuru Peak, signs the same official record book at the Tanzania Park Ranger Station upon exiting at Marangu Gate. That tends to show the locals don't care where on Kilimanjaro you call summit, as long as it's on the top. The authorities took exception to Gene's special request that he be taken down by gurney. The impact on his knees from the stress of summit day, including hiking to Uhuru, left him seriously injured. If the unbearable pain of bone on bone grinding in both joints was not enough, he was convinced any further rupture to the tissue would cripple him for life.

Back at the Kibo Hut, Gene made all necessary inquiries to find out if he could pay a porter for a gurney ride down to Morangu Gate using one of the four gurneys stacked outside the hut. I thought it was a good idea to save his knees. Dollars go a long way on Kilimanjaro, but they informed him in no uncertain terms the only way you get a gurney ride is if you are dead. That being the case, he took the brutal walk down which left him so he never hiked again.

I was drinking a Coke outside the Marangu Gate, sitting on the steps of the ranger station the next afternoon, when I spotted Gene coming down the path to the finish line. He walked over and stopped directly in front of me. I hadn't talked to Gene for more than five minutes the entire time we had been in Africa, so this was a surprise. Right out the blue he says:

"I know things can change. But I've been watching you and D'Arcy, and it appears you guys are very much in love. I hope things work out. But here's the deal. One of the benefits I get as a retired judge is to marry people. It's a perk," he laughed and went on, "If you two ever decide to get married, my wife and I have done major renovations to our home in Tahoe. You'd be welcome to use it. We could do the ceremony in our back yard. I'd love to do the honors," he said, and gave me his warmest smile.

I could tell he'd been thinking about that for a long time. Thinking, all those miles coming down the trail.

Pounding down the final leg of the journey from Horombo, his knees swollen with fluids in a futile attempt to protect his joints. The thought of conducting a marriage ceremony must have soothed his pain. But a marriage ceremony forged from the snows of Kilimanjaro would give it the special meaning it deserves; and a bit of glamour for the already overachieving judge and for us.

Right in his back yard, I thought. I envisioned a rectangular backyard, manicured green grass with a picket redwood fence, typical of the small homes built along the lake front of South Lake Tahoe.

To be the Municipal Court Judge of that tiny Sierra hamlet for thirty years was a legal coup for any judge wanting to live in the most magnificent Alpine region in California. It's located contiguous to the most beautiful 560 acres of gambling casinos in America, on the Nevada side of Lake Tahoe, at Stateline, NV.

"That's very nice of you. We'll have to see how things go," I replied.

Endless Days, Endless Nights

We got married in his backyard 485 days later. I could not have been more wrong in my vision of what he was offering when he offered his home. He had a yard off the back of his house all right, but there was no fence. It was an open area, straight to the sky-blue waters of the lake. It went far beyond the pine trees, pine needles and pinecones, reaching out to the wet meadow of flowering yellowcress, and beyond that to the beach. His back yard was made up of soccer fields of Tahoe fauna.

That afternoon D'Arcy and I pledged our vows forever. Later that night we got the penthouse suite in the top western corner of Harrah's Hotel and Casino. It was one of those lucky nights. Every time we passed a roulette wheel, while bouncing from the crap tables to blackjack, I would put a hundred-dollar bill on red or black depending on how we felt. Every time the wheel stopped, it paid me back two hundred dollars. We laughed loudly and moved on.

After we got thrown out of one casino for videotaping our fun, we crossed the street to Harrah's where I inquired about the suite. They wanted $1,500.00 for the night and not a penny less. I tried to turn on the charm and put my negotiation skills to work. It's easier to do so with a wad of cash in your pocket to bolster the plea. "We just got married. It's 9:00 o'clock, the night's half over." Didn't matter, it was like trying to charm a rattler. But I was on a mission, and after speaking with the manager, I finally got it for $900.

The suite was a masterpiece of decadence. Windows the size of movie screens jetted over the lake. The sunrise brought dawn rays that refracted like crystals off the water. Bedrooms had beds the size of spaceships. There were enough TVs and telephones to fill up a *Best Buy*. The remote control was heavier than a computer. The carpet so thick we made love on it a dozen times. There was a his, hers, theirs, and anybody else's bathroom. After Kibo Hut, we were finally back on top of the world.

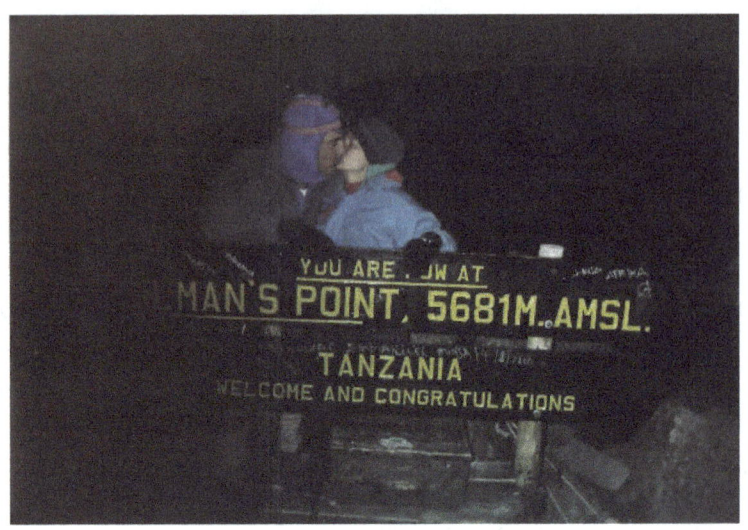

Summit sunrise!

MT. KILIMANJARO

D'Arcy and me at Mandara Hut

The Gang

SANTA BARBARA, CALIFORNIA (2015)
21.
A Stroke is Upon Me

On the 2nd of August 2015, I had a massive stroke. The last words I remember my wife saying were, "Are you messing with me?" It didn't take her but a few seconds to see I wasn't kidding. I was vacating my body, shutting down and non-responsive to everything. She called 911, put the dogs in the bedroom, then ran outside to flag down the ambulance.

They were only a few blocks away. She could hear them coming with sirens blaring, coming up the street and screeching to a halt outside my house. Three paramedics jumped out and at the direction of my wife ran up to the third floor where they found me still at my desk. My last conscious thought came to mind as the men approached, taking their medical instruments out of their bags, and bombarding me with questions, "They're so young…well, of course they are, who else could run up three flights of stairs with the expectation of carrying me down…" and then I was gone.

Fortunately, there was an elevator right behind me. They squeezed me in the elevator still in my chair, then put me in the ambulance as quickly as possible and we were at Cottage Hospital in a matter of five minutes. This was good for me because speed counts when a blood clot has stopped the flow of nutrients to the brain. No blood to the brain has nasty results. The worse being you can die. Or perhaps the worst is you don't die but are left to live only able to say, "Mammy, mammy, mammy, mammy," for the rest of your life.

I had no idea what happened to me. I was gone for two days—no dreams or light shows, or ethereal experiences. But when I came back, it was like Christmas morning. The first person I see is D'Arcy, then my daughter Aurora, what the hell is going on? I was surprised to see them. But I couldn't speak because something had been rammed down my throat, and my hands were tied to the railings on the sides of my bed. Once I got rid of those shackles, I was ready to find out what was happening. And the first thing I found out was I couldn't remember D'Arcy's name.

It turned out that as soon as I arrived at the hospital I had been whisked into emergency surgery. I had the type of stroke where the clot formed in my heart had been caused by atrial fibrillation. It broke loose and flowed up and lodged in my brain, where it clogged the artery, stopping the flow of blood and nearly killing me. But the clot didn't have time to kill me because of a new drug called tPA (tissue plasminogen activator) or *giant anticoagulant*, which is the gold standard for all ischemic stroke patients. That is, if you're lucky enough to get the drug.

The key to getting tPA is getting to the hospital within three hours. And there must also be a doctor talented enough to perform a thrombectomy. You must have it administered within three hours of the first symptoms of your stroke. That's the cut off, any later in time and the hospital runs the risk of devastating results, such as intracerebral hemorrhage or "bleeding in your brain."

I pity the poor bastard who arrives five minutes after the three-hour limitation. Maybe he's been waiting for help on a gurney, busy nurses running by while his time runs out, or the man who lives alone and isn't discovered until tomorrow, or the wife who doesn't recognize the symptoms and decides he can sleep it off, or the farmer who lives too far outside the city, or the city that isn't big enough to keep a surgeon for a "mechanical thrombectomy" on call. In fact, they keep statistics on this sort of thing. Of the 43 percent of patients having access to tPA, only 3 percent end up using it.

If you had a stroke, and there was one thing you could do for yourself, you would want to get to the hospital soon enough to be eligible for tPA. It works as a super anticoagulant that might dissolve the clot itself to improve the blood flow. But if you're like me, the clot will be too stubborn, and you will need a doctor trained to perform a mechanical thrombectomy. These doctors can remove these blood clots by sending a clot extraction device called a "stent retriever" to the site of the blocked blood vessel in the middle of my brain.

To remove *my* clot, the doctor navigated this catheter, starting from the jugular on the right side of my neck, working his way up the clogged artery to the site of the massive clot. When he reached the site in the left middle of the cerebral artery, the stent retriever opened up and grabbed the clot by using special suction tubes that allowed the retriever to trap the clot in its clutches. The doctor then navigated the catheter back down the artery and out the jugular in my neck. It was impressive. But this procedure can only be done after a patient receives tPA, and they must receive it one hour before the thrombectomy.

My doctor showed me a picture of his handy work several weeks after the thrombectomy was performed, and only at my insistence. I was amazed to see a small log. It was one inch long, black, and in the shape of a cylinder, just like an artery. He wound his stent retriever up into my brain so he could pull out the log jamming up my blood flow. I would otherwise be dead. What can I say? Thank you.

I got medical assistance as fast as anyone could get it and I still I didn't know my wife's name. Within thirty minutes of being in the ambulance and driven to emergency, I was receiving tPA intravenously and I still didn't know the day or the month that it occurred. I could remember September and July, but I couldn't remember the month of August for a couple of weeks. Nor could I remember the word "hammock," as I sat staring at the picture of one. And I still can't add or subtract small change.

Thank God for neural plasticity. Doctors used to believe that once brain tissue was damaged it was no good. But now we know the brain is more like a giant ant hill. If the ants' pathways get disrupted, they will find new pathways leading back to the same place, given time. And that's the same way the brain functions. If your neuron connections get disrupted or damaged due to a stroke or injury, they will reorganize themselves over time to create new pathways leading to the same place. The brain is always at work, changing to new stimuli.

But the brain isn't the only organ to take a beating during a stroke. It can take a strong 200-pound man and leave him 150-pound weakling. That's what happened to me. This evil spirit that came from my own heart stretched me out and beat my back by stomping on it with what felt like hobnail boots, then kicked and kneed me in the kidney and spine, taking my right leg and pulling and twisting it in the socket, swinging me in circles with no mercy. I didn't feel any of this as it happened. This was the wretch I felt like afterward, and still... I felt lucky.

I didn't know if I had a pot to piss in. I couldn't speak and was frustrated; but my wife and daughter were there. And there was nothing else I cared about. I didn't know if there was anything else to care about. A feeding tube was shoved down my gullet, my hands were tied, and all I could do was feel fortunate. I remember crying, I was so happy, or was it luck, or simple destiny. I didn't know where I was, or what the problem could be, all I knew was I had everything I needed.

Thus, I began the road to recovery. The first thing to deal with was the pain in my lower back. It made the blisters I suffered on Aconcagua feel like I was celebrating my tenth birthday. This was a deep muscle wound centered between my spine and my right hip—as though a lead ball had been shot there. When I tried to sit up this ball would explode with something so vile it struck a nerve that reached throughout my body and reverberated from head to toe. I sat lopsided on the side of my bed, one hand under my butt, tears streaming down my face, because if I moved, I'd cause more agony. I couldn't move. I'd sit like that for twenty minutes before being helped into the wheelchair.

But no one could tell me what was wrong with my back. It was as though that's just part of the experience of having a stroke. It comes with the territory. Once you've had a stroke, all diagnosis for any previous malady is off the table because you're considered living on borrowed time.

That pain subsided in about three weeks so I could walk, but it felt more like three years. I was truly lucky not to be permanently paralyzed. Originally, my entire right side was paralyzed, from mouth to foot. But I began to make a *remarkable recovery* from day to day(so says my medical record). They put me in rehab with other stroke victims where I learned to count my lucky stars. I never knew a stroke could be so devastating.

Patients would try as hard as they could to get a spoonful of something to their mouth and it would drop off before it got there. Some were unable to feed themselves, others would throw up at the table. They would try to talk but it would make no sense. They'd fall out of their wheelchairs and send their family home in tears over their total disability. Where once there was a man, there is an infant in need. The whole rehab scene was extraordinarily sad, so I was happy to be heading home.

The interesting thing about having a stroke is you don't know how bad you are until it's pointed out. You don't know what you don't know. For example, I thought I could tell you the name of the highest mountain on each continent, until you asked me to name them.

"Well, let's see, there's McKinley, that's in Alaska which is on…it's on the North, the northern part. There's the lower 48, and it's not there…On Africa? I can do this…it's Illimani, no it's Frazer…no, it starts with a K…Kilimanjaro?"

But wow! Neural plasticity takes care of all that. It takes time, however, and the help of the psychological, vocational, occupational, and physical therapists who were all very helpful. But one thing they couldn't help me with was neural whimpicity.

That's where with every conversation you have with another person, if it's an emotionally charged subject, like you're discussing a news story or a scene in the movies, and it has the slightest passionate nuance, your eyes not only well up with tears, but will flow uncontrollably, streaming down your cheeks in embarrassment. You become veiled in a body of tears over any little thing.

The baby giraffe at the zoo is named Chad after a long-time benefactor, or the word 'Grand' is explored in the 'Grandparent' relationship. A little girl is lost, and the father is broken hearted, or a mother is elated over her son graduating from high school. It doesn't matter. A juvenile delinquent is honoring his coach, or a ten-year-old throws a party for a cop. The stroke victim comes overloaded with compassion. A young man finally gets to play in a football game, or an autistic girl finally makes a basket in the basketball game. The person that suffered a stroke is feeling all of it.

I know this runs true amongst stroke victims because it's a standard part of the therapy. They warn you against this phenomenon of tears. It's not really crying; it's more like weeping because the tears well up and overflow without a sound. The psychologist tells you that "your defense system has been attacked, and that defense is momentarily broken, and unable to filter out the real emotion from whatever this other over-sensitivity could be."

I asked the psychologist if he could help explain this "over-sensation," because it was playing havoc with my life. I was getting upset and saddened by life, too many people were getting hurt for no reason, too much unexplained death, all done by happenstance. And then there's beauty, children were saved, heroes lived among us, and justice occurred in the strangest ways. "When is this going to stop, because I'm tired of crying my eyes out over this over-sensation!"

The psychologist looked at me as though I just let out the biggest fart ever heard in the world. I remember his face squinted up around his nose, as his mouth grimaced at the edge and turned down at the corners. He apparently was uncomfortable when he said, "It gets better, rest assured, it gets better."

My surgeon, Dr. Taylor, wrote in my medical records that I was "making a remarkable recovery." I can't help but thank my mountain climbing experience for that. What do you think would have happened to me had I previously not climbed Everest, Denali, Aconcagua, Kilimanjaro, Mont Blanc, the Matterhorn, Mt. Cook and …Vinson Massif? Well, there was no Vinson Massif, but I'm not dead yet. More on that, later. I like to think climbing in those mountains did something to build my physical stamina to endure pain. Climbing at altitudes causes severe pain throughout your entire body due to oxygen deprivation.

The skill of enduring pain would have helped me get over the clot removal that allowed me to heal. The last time I was in great shape was 2006. I spent the summer hiking the trails between Cold Springs and Romero Canyon in the foothills behind Santa Barbara. I hiked every path, up, over, crossways, and down until I'd hiked them all. And as I did so I thought, what great exercise this is, hopefully it will pay off.

But then I had a series of setbacks. First there was the pacemaker for my heart, which was no small adjustment with the SA node snipped. Then there were ten years of misdiagnosed hemochromatosis, necessitating endless blood draws wrongfully prescribed. After that my right hip had to be replaced, followed four months later by my left hip being replaced, which led to anemia; and then I got pneumonia, over and over which hospitalized me a week at a time. This brought me up to my sixty-fifth birthday, thank goodness, because when I got the stroke in

August, I was on the dole at Medi-Care, and they picked up the $175,000 tab.

Dr. Taylor told me I had one year from the date of my stroke to get better, and after that, I'd be as good as it gets. After one year, he told me, I should have no expectation of getting better from the stroke, both physically and mentally — as though there was something magical about 365 days that would bring the recovery period to an end. No more neuroplasticity or physical therapy will make you better. If your surgeon told you the same thing about recovery time, tell them from me they are full of excrement.

I don't know why the surgeon said that, but he did, several times. Maybe it was meant to limit his personal liability as a surgeon in case of a lawsuit. Or perhaps it was meant to inspire me to work hard with my therapists for at least a year. Or maybe, it was just meant to put an end to all this stroke business. But in any case, it's not very encouraging news.

What happens to your body after that year is over Doc? Does the stroke, with all the calamities it causes, just go away, and you're stuck with the residual effects, say, a bum leg, or a crook in your back, or a mind that doesn't work right? You can't get better?

The answer to these questions is no, no, no! You're not stuck with anything because you've got years ahead to change your condition. It's now been ten years since my stroke and I'm still working with the neural plasticity to get rid of the neural whimpicity. It's not easy. Trying to shake those lingering effects of a stroke can hold you back from becoming everything you want to be. You don't want to be just another stroke victim. But that's what I am, and I'm proud of it. But sometimes, I wonder what I don't know about myself.

I haven't climbed a mountain in twenty-five years. I never doubted my ability to climb Vinson Massif. I could have run up it in a day or two. But there's no possibility of climbing it now. And it's not because of the exorbitant price. I tried to hike up Romero Canyon, my old stomping ground, to see how far I'd get, and it ended in complete failure. I barely got a mile up the path before I collapsed with pain rifling through my back. The debilitating effect of old age, or weakness in my spine resulting from the stroke? The question is: can it be cured? The spinal cord stimulator I had was no help. It was like being thrown a life preserver when a Great White has you in its jaws.

On my last birthday I turned 75 years old. I'm still working to be in the best shape of my life. Right now, I've shrunk three inches and am 168 pounds of climbing fury. And what I lack in fury I make up for with pondering.

I'm still recovering and enjoying my life — a life made possible by marrying D'Arcy twenty-five years ago. I have climbed the highest mountain on six of the seven continents. Though Everest was one summit that eluded me, D'Arcy was not. She was my Seventh Summit.

ABOUT THE AUTHOR

MARK S. CORNWALL lives in Summerland, California. After graduating from UCSB in philosophy, he went to Alaska to work in the woods as a logger. He married, had a child, went to law school, divorced, then climbed six of the *Seven Summits*, the last one being Kilimanjaro, which he climbed with his wife, D'Arcy, in the year 2000.

Between then and now, Mark filled his life with adventures. Writing came later in life. The only "writing" Mark did as a trial attorney for 33 years, were briefs for the State and Federal Appellate Courts. But as great as that success was, it was put to an immediate end by a stroke in 2015. That's when Mark was set free from his legal obligations to write what he always wanted to write about: true travel and adventure stories.

"I always dreamt of being a writer but was too busy writing as an attorney. Legal briefs are not written, they're regurgitated. It wasn't until the stroke forced me to push for the stars that I found my literary voice."

www.ingramcontent.com/pod-product-compliance
Lightning Source LLC
Chambersburg PA
CBHW071620170426
43195CB00038B/1494